The Financial Sector of the American Economy

EDITED BY
STUART BRUCHEY

A GARLAND SERIES

Money and Consumer Durable Spending

BY

CHRISTOPHER BROWN

GARLAND PUBLISHING, INC.
NEW YORK & LONDON
1993

Library of Congress Cataloging-in-Publication Data

Brown, Christopher, 1955-
Money and consumer durable spending / by Christopher Brown.
p. cm. — (Financial sector of the American economy)
ISBN 0-8153-1211-3 (alk. paper)
1. Consumers—United States. 2. Durable goods, Consumer—United States. 3. Monetary policy—United States. I. Title. II. Series.
HC110.C6B74 1993
339.4'7'0973—dc20 92-34573
CIP

Printed on acid-free, 250-year-life paper
Manufactured in the United States of America

Contents

List of Illustrations

Preface

As the final draft of this work was being prepared for publication, economists were debating whether the recession, which according to the National Bureau of Economic Research (NBER) commenced in July 1990, had finally run its course. Evaluated solely by its length, the 1990-1992 recession was certain to rank as the most severe of the postwar era. Predictably, economists were supplying a myriad of explanations for the most recent business cycle contraction. Economists representing a wide range of methodological and ideological persuasions appeared to be in agreement, however, on at least one point: The sharp increase in private and public sector debt in the expansionary phase following the 1981-1982 recession was a significant contributing factor to the present slump in economic activity. Indeed, William Seidman, former chairman of the FDIC, described the 1990-1992 recession as a "balance sheet-adjustment recession."

This book is a revised version of a dissertation presented for the doctoral degree in economics in 1989. It was written against the backdrop of an historically unprecedented build-up of household indebtedness which occurred in the U.S. between 1983 and 1989. The central question posed by the study is straightforward: Is there any connection between the pervasive use of debt by households to finance the purchase consumer durable goods and the observed cyclical volatility of the consumer durable goods series? The answer provided in the forthcoming pages is an unequivocal yes.

Much has been written about the consumer credit industry as well as the causal relationship between credit flows and the level of production and employment. Martha Olney, for instance, has recently argued that, where the automobile industry is concerned, credit has served mainly as a production-smoothing device.[1] A more comprehensive view of things is taken here. For example, it is asserted that the manufacturing and marketing of consumer durable goods on a massive scale in the twentieth century *necessarily* required the concomitant development of systems which ensured the regularized, uninterrupted flow of installment credit extensions to the household sector. The growth of the installment credit industry and the liberalization of social attitudes in regard to household borrowing are interpreted as economic and institutional adjustments to the problem of income maldistribution--a problem which threatened to stall the development of consumer durable goods industries in their inchoate phase. Moreover, the crucial role of installment lending in sustaining the demand for consumer durable goods has implanted sources of cyclical instability in the macroeconomic system which have been generally overlooked by contemporary business cycle theorists. The general plan of the plan of the book is to systematically describe these sources of instability and to evaluate their relative importance in past business cycle fluctuations in the U.S.

With regard to the methodology employed in this book, those who insist that economic analysis be firmly grounded in the standard choice-theoretic optimization framework will be disappointed. The microfoundations of the work are clearly Marshallian as opposed to Walrasian. The influence of Keynes and the leaders of the contemporary Post Keynesian school of economics, including Paul Davidson, Hyman Minsky, and Basil Moore, should be obvious to the reader. The analysis presented in the following pages could be accurately described as Post Keynesian in the sense of treating money as something that is conceptually and pratically distinquishable from "all other commodities."

A few comments about the relevance of the principal arguments contained in this volume to the problem raised earlier, i.e., the current economic slump, are appropriate here. First, the book attempts to describe how a sustained boom in spending for durable goods can result in the deterioration of household balance sheets, and therefore create

[1]Martha L. Olney. "Credit as a Production Smoothing Device: The Case of Automobiles," *Journal of Economic History*, 49, June 1989, 377-391.

conditions for a subsequent decline in consumer spending. This principle is an extension of Professor Minksy's debt deflation hypothesis to the household sector.

A troubling, if not shocking, aspect of the current recession is the high incidence of permanent plant closings, corporate reorganizations and downsizings, and the growing phenomena of contingent or "just-in-time" employment. As is argued in Chapter 3, the practice of buying goods on installment is ultimately based on the confidence of both debtors and creditors as to the predictability and/or stability of future income flows. It appears that Americans of nearly every income and occupational group are facing a heightened level of income and job uncertainty as a result of the structural changes taking place today. The increased uncertainty is likely to be manifest in the more judicious use of installment credit by households and the lengthening of replacement cycles for automobiles and other durable goods.

Jonesboro, Arkansas
September, 1992

CHRISTOPHER BROWN

Acknowledgements

I would like to express my gratitude and appreciation to the many people who have assisted me and without whose help this study would not have been possible.

Professor Paul Davidson of the University of Tennessee was of enormous help in shaping the focus and the structure of the study. His many valuable comments pointed out shortcomings of the thesis and suggested tangible ways of improving it. I am also indebted to Professors Ann Mayhew and Hans Jensen of the University of Tennessee, both of whom read the manuscript and offered helpful suggestions. In addition, I wish to thank Professor Stuart Bruchey of Columbia University, who read the manuscript and recommended its publication to Garland Publishing Inc.

I also wish to express my thanks to Holly Bell of the Department of Economics, University of Tennessee as well as the Business Computer Resources Group, University of Tennessee, for translating computer discs of an earlier version of the manuscript.

Thanks are due to Professor John Kaminarides and the Office of Business Research at Arkansas State University for extensive help in the preparation of the final manuscript. Special gratitude is due Ms. Tonia Harrison for the many hours of expert technical assistance she provided. Professor Steve Replogle of Arkansas State University offered troubleshooting services in the preparation of computer graphics for which I am grateful. Kevin Lawrence assisted in preparing the index.

I also wish to thank Claudia Hirsch, Anita Vanca, and Jon Oestrich for editorial assistance.

Finally, I am indebted to Professor C.K. McFarland of Arkansas State University, who gave selflessly in reading the entire manuscript and in offering many constructive suggestions.

Money and Consumer Durable Spending

Chapter 1

Introduction

A basic problem in business cycle theory concerns the manner in which monetary variables enter into the determination of real sector magnitudes such as real output and employment. That is, to what extent and under what circumstances are changes in monetary variables, however defined, nonneutral with respect to the physical flow of goods and services produced in the economy? Much of the existing literature in monetary theory is concerned with the nature of the transmission mechanism of money to real variables. For the conduct of stabilization policy, it would be useful to know which components of aggregate expenditure are sensitive to monetary influences and the precise nature of the linkages of money and effective demand. For the critics of countercyclical demand management, evidence of the destabilizing effects of erratic changes in the rate of monetary expansion strengthens the case for policy rules.

The analytical foundation of the Keynesian income-expenditure approach to business cycle theory is the principle of effective demand which can be stated briefly as follows: In the time interval in which the social capacity to produce goods and services is taken as given within narrow limits, the extent to which existing productive capacity is utilized is determined by the volume of effective demand. Theoretical and empirical articulation of the principle of effective demand logically requires the decomposition of the aggregate demand function and inquiry into the determinants of the various categories of aggregate expenditure. Investigations into the importance of monetary phenomena for the level or stability of effective demand have typically been conducted in the formulation of investment theory. Articulators of the Keynesian paradigm have generally found it reasonable to suppose that monetary variables are important to the extent that they impinge on the category of spending defined as investment. Consequently, research pertaining to the transmission mechanism conducted in the framework of the Keynesian income-expenditure approach has typically involved modeling of the interest rate-investment linkage.[1] Less attention has been devoted to the monetary determinants of consumption expenditure. Household consumption expenditure accounts for greater than half of the total expenditure for final goods and services, or gross national product, each year. Moreover, household spending for goods and services, and most importantly spending for durable goods, exhibits a considerable degree of volatility in time series data (see Figure 1-1). The durable series is strongly procyclical and, with the exception of residential construction and producer goods sales, shows the greatest degree of amplitude of any of the spending series in post World War II business cycle expansions and contractions. The standard deviation of the growth rate of durable sales is 8.5%, compared to a standard deviation for nondurables and services of 1.4%. (The standard deviations for newly constructed residential housing and producer durable goods are, respectively, 8.8% and 14.2%). The evidence indicates that the volatility of household spending for durable goods is at the very least a contributing factor to the observed instability of effective demand.[2] Determining the extent of the impact of monetary forces on household spending could partly explain the short run instability of the consumption function and contribute to an understanding of cyclical fluctuations in general. To that end, a theory of the role of money in the consumption function will be developed.

The argument contained herein is that monetary forces influence the volume of household spending in a direct and powerful way which has been generally overlooked in theoretical and empirical treatments of the consumption function. Specifically, money matters in the consumption function because a significant, and secularly increasing, proportion of aggregate household spending is financed with bank-created money. The crucial importance of monetary phenomena in the consumption function thus derives from the peculiar role of financial institutions in mature monetary economies.

The primary function of financial institutions consists in the creation and sale of monetary claims which enable debtors to obtain disposal over goods. That is, commercial banks are engaged in the activity of creating purchasing power which does not derive from the

Figure 1-1

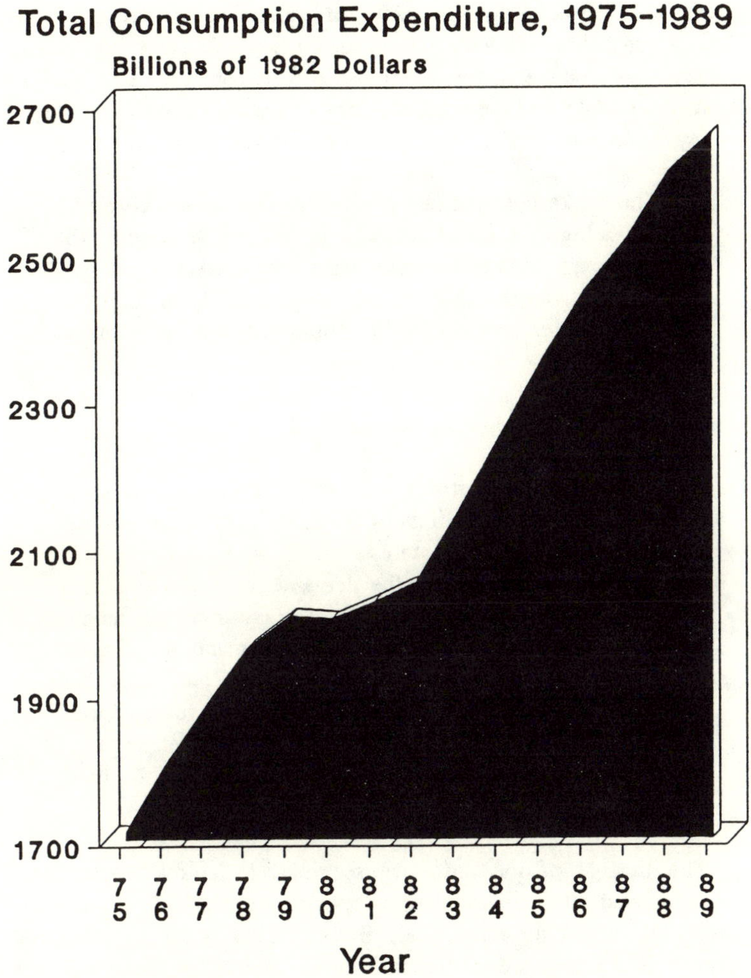

Source: *Business Conditions Digest*, series 231.

production and sale of goods in the current period or in past periods. To paraphrase Schumpeter, bank-created money represents a "fictitious claim" to the total social product, i.e., individuals obtain monetary claims to goods and services based not on current or past earnings but rather in prospect of future income flows.[3] This characterization of commercial bank functions represents no radical departure from the picture which emerges from most money and banking textbooks and is generally consistent with the views of writers as diverse as Irving Fisher, Von Mises, Simons, Cameron, Gurley and Shaw, and Harry Johnson. Moreover, the relationship between the activities of commercial banks and the level of effective demand is well recognized by Keynesian economists. For example, Keynes wrote:

> The banks hold the key position in the transition from a lower to a higher scale of activity. If they refuse to relax, the growing congestion of the short term loan market or the new issue market, as the case may be, will inhibit the improvement, no matter how thrifty the public purpose turns out to be.[4]

In a similar vein, Davidson has commented:

> If, for example, institutional barriers, imperfections in the money market or operations of financial institutions restrain changes in the rate of interest which would otherwise be associated with changes in the demand for finance, at any given level of employment and output (assuming the money market cleared before the increase in demand for finance occurred), then credit rationing will prevail, and individual firms are prevented from making their "wants" for increased capital goods per period effective in the market by their inability to borrow money to use to pay for delivery on offer contracts.[5]

The linkage of the monetary sector and the real sector has, however, most often been viewed as operating exclusively through the activity of producing units, i.e., firms. That is to say financial institutions are engaged in the activity of creating monetary claims which facilitate the hiring of productive factors by

Figure 1-2

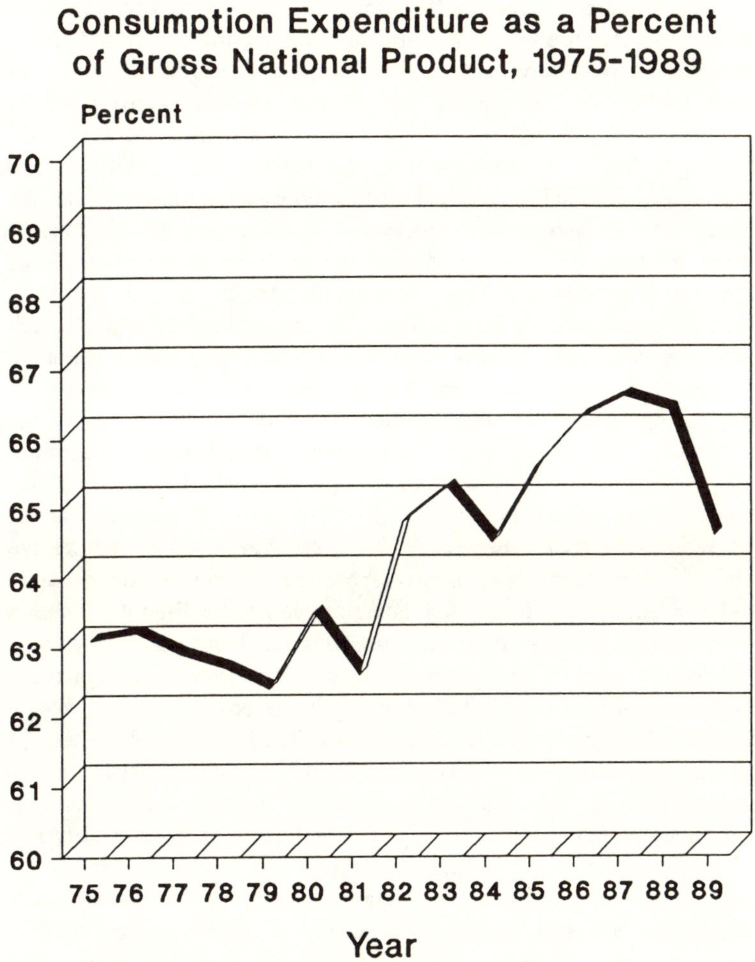

Source: *Economic Report of the President.*

firms. Standard approaches to the theory of the consumption function typically abstract from the linkage between household spending and bank-created monetary claims. It is my contention that the theory of the consumption function needs to be reexamined in light of some basic institutional changes in the postwar era.

There has been a change in the pattern of household expenditure in favor of big ticket durable items. The purchase of a big ticket consumer durable good often involves a cash flow problem. Households acquire consumer durable goods in order to gain disposal over a stream of services yielded by such durables in the course of their useful life. However, durable goods manufactures typically require payment in full prior to, or at least at a point coincident with, the beginning of the useful life of the products they market. The availability of installment credit enables households to smooth out the stream of cash disbursements necessary for the acquisition of a durable good so that the flow of disbursements bears a more desirable relationship to the flow of services yielded by the durable good. In fact, the manufacturing and marketing of consumer durable goods such as automobiles on a massive scale would hardly be possible if not for the existence of financial institutions which stand ready to supply purchasing power to the household sector. Furthermore, the appearance and rapid growth of institutions such as finance companies and the increased participation of commercial banks in the market for consumer loans have resulted in much greater accessibility of households to credit markets. There has developed an aggressive attempt to persuade households to become borrowers that is quite independent of the effort to sell them durable goods. Figure 1-2 shows one measure of consumer debt--installment debt outstanding as a percent of personal disposable income--which indicates a sharp increase in the intensity of household borrowing in the postwar period.

The thesis may be restated as follows: The fundamental connection of the monetary sector and household spending consists in the accessibility of households to bank-created money. The volume of consumer spending is therefore partly contingent upon the ability and motivation of financial institutions such as commercial banks, savings and loans, credit unions, and finance companies to extend liquid purchasing power to the household sector. A parallel consideration is the willingness of households to incur debt liabilities. These two factors interact to determine the stock of household debt outstanding at

Figure 1-3

Consumer Durable Spending, 1975-1989

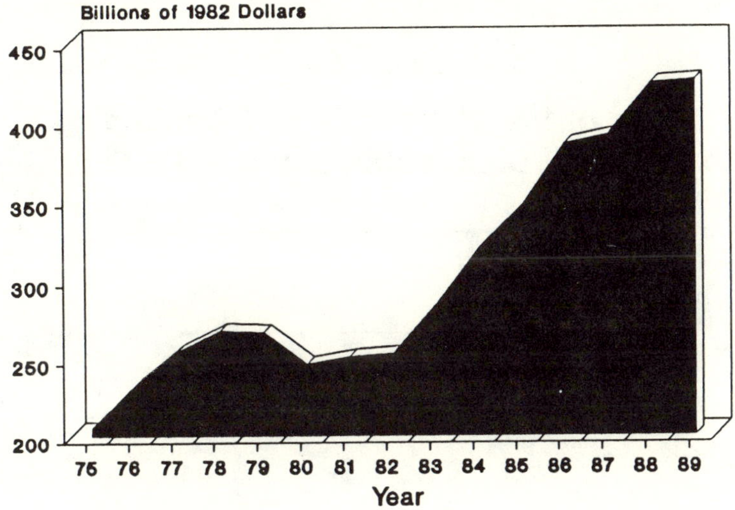

Source: *Business Conditions Digest*, series 233.

a point in time, or the rate of change of household indebtedness in the current quarter or year. Conceptually, if we hold the partial derivatives of consumption expenditure with respect to both income and wealth constant, the level of aggregate household spending will change in direct proportion to the volume of new credits extended to the household sector.

This then gives rise to important questions: Can the cyclical behavior of consumer spending be explained by a breakdown in the mechanisms which provide a regularized flow of bank-created monetary claims to the household sector? That is to say could it be the case that a slump in consumer spending might be partly the result of contractionary monetary policy or a liquidity crisis in the banking system which results in a drastic curtailment of consumer lending activity? Furthermore, is the procyclical movement of the durable series in any way related to the psychological attitude toward debt on the part of households? That is, is the attitude toward debt liabilities subject to sudden change, and if so, what are the implications for the stability of consumer spending? These questions form the central focus of the thesis. The study concentrates on durable sales for two reasons:

Figure 1-4

Ratio of Installment Debt Outstanding to Personal Disposable Income, 1975-1989

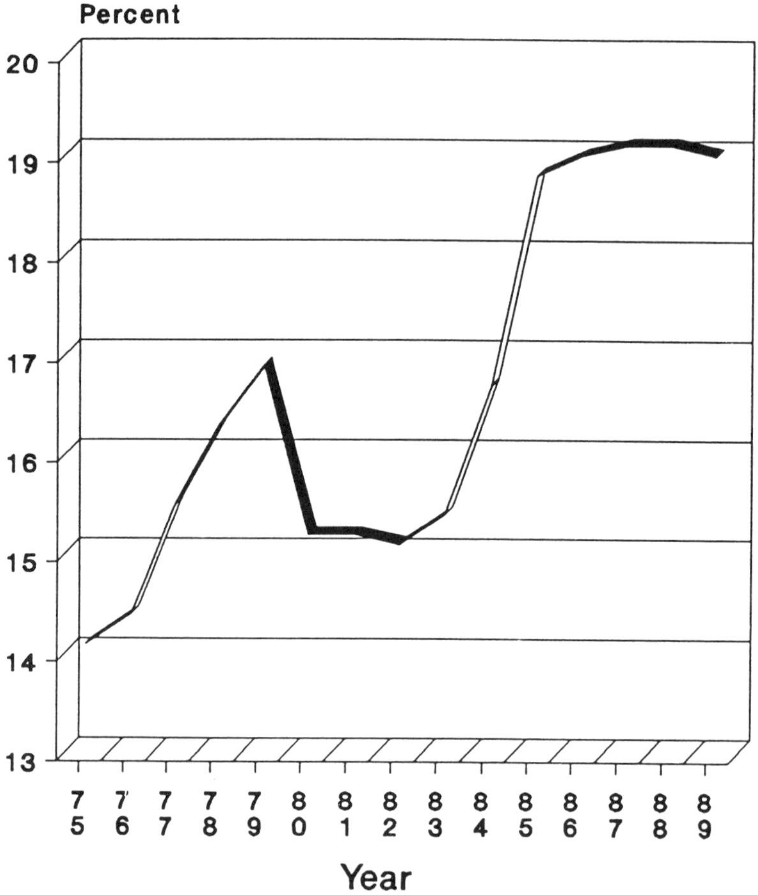

Source: *Business Conditions Digest*, series 66 and 225.

First, the short run instability of the consumption function is almost entirely attributable to the volatility of durable spending. Secondly, most household non-mortgage debt is used to finance the purchase of goods with a useful life of greater than one year.

Two potential sources of instability related to the role of money in the consumption function will be investigated. The first concerns the willingness of households to incur debt obligations and is defined as "the attitude toward indebtedness." The second is the ability and motivation on the part of financial institutions to accommodate the household demand for finance and is referred to as "credit availability" effects. These phenomena are analyzed in the general framework of partial equilibrium analysis.

Chapter 2 will review the literature pertaining to the linkage of money and consumer spending and contrast received interpretations with the thesis outlined above. Chapter 3 contains the theoretical core of the dissertation and examines the set of factors which collectively determine the household demand for finance. Supply-side conditions in consumer installment credit markets are the subject of Chapter 4. The relationship between consumer credit expansion, consumer durable spending and inflation is the subject of Chapter 5. Chapter 6 investigates the relationship between Federal Reserve policy and consumer durable spending. Finally, conclusions and policy implications are stated in Chapter 7.

NOTES

1. Frequently cited works include Jorgenson and Stevenson (1967), Tobin (1969), and Brechling (174).

2. The term "durable goods" corresponds to "consumer durables" as defined in the National Income Accounts. A durable is defined as a consumer good with a useful life of three years or more. The category is composed mainly of motor vehicles and parts (45%) and furniture and household equipment (35%). Housing is excluded.

3. Schumpeter (1954), p. 107.

4. Keynes (1973), p. 688.

5. Davidson (1978), p. 184.

Chapter 2

Standard Approaches to the Money-Consumer Spending Linkage

There is a large body of scholarship concerning the relationship of money to consumption expenditure. Yet comparatively little research has been conducted along the lines suggested in Chapter 1, that is, on the importance of monetary phenomena for consumption and the crucial role of the commercial banking system as supplier of purchasing power to the household sector. Standard approaches to the monetary transmission mechanism can be roughly classified under three headings: Interest rate effects, net wealth effects, and portfolio adjustment effects. This chapter will review this literature and contrast these interpretations with the approach outlined in Chapter 1. In addition, there will be a discussion of the usual treatment of the problem of "credit availability effects" in the market for consumer loans.

2.1 INTEREST RATE EFFECTS

It is generally agreed that it is within the scope of the powers of the monetary authority to target interest rates.[1] The immediate effect of an open market operation is to impinge on the prices and yields of a particular class of debt instruments such as short dated Treasury issues. The yields on a wide spectrum of debt instruments will generally follow in sympathy depending upon the elasticity of substitution among the various classes of debt instruments.[2]

Assuming that the monetary authority does in fact exert an influence on the complex of interest rates, what is the theoretical justification for positing interest rates as a determinant of consumption spending? This is a particularly confusing issue in the orthodox literature, which seeks to formulate aggregate behavioral relationships based on the neoclassical optimization problem of individual economic agents.[3] One thing is clear, however; the interest rate figures into the household optimization calculus as one price in a vector of relative prices. What is unclear is this: If the interest rate is a price, what is it the price of? Is the interest rate the price of credit? Or is it something like a shadow price which reveals the relative price of current consumption measured in terms of foregone future consumption? Perhaps more importantly, does the question of the interest rate as the "price of something" have any bearing on the importance of interest rates, or monetary phenomena in general, in the determination of consumer spending?

Orthodox practitioners of economics seek a theory which is capable of explaining changing patterns of household spending, or changes in the absolute volume of household expenditure in a particular time interval, in terms of optimizing responses of economic agents to changes in relative prices and endowments given the assumption of stable preference functions. To incorporate the effect of interest rate variability on the optimal solution to a choice theoretic optimization problem, the Fisherine multiperiod optimization framework is typically deployed. Interest rates are taken to be significant at the micro level only in the case where agents have a multiperiod planning horizon and an intertemporal budget constraint. This conclusion follows from the usual assumption of monotonicity, i.e., "more is preferred to less." If agents have a single-period decision frontier, a necessary condition for maximization of the objective function requires agents to allocate all income and wealth for the purchase of goods and services during the period. In the multiperiod case, monotonicity only requires that the intertemporal budget constraint be exhausted which does not preclude the possibility of borrowing and lending activities. Given this scenario, prevailing interest rates enter into the household maximization problem to the extent that they influence the relative price of consumption today vis á vis consumption in future periods. For example, suppose that, other things being equal, there is an increase in the interest rate. This will result in an increase in the relative price of current consumption measured in terms of foregone future consumption. If current and future consumption are substitutes, an increase in the interest rate can be expected to induce a contraction of current spending as agents substitute future for current consumption in response to the relative price change. The magnitude of the change in spending depends on the change in the interest rate and the elasticity of substitution between current and future consumption.[4] Conversely, a monetary stimulus can be expected to induce an increase in current spending by putting downward pressure on the price of current consumption, once again measured in terms of foregone future consumption. Analytically, the prevailing interest rate can be treated as the discount rate applied to future income flows. Or, to put it differently, the interest rate gives the terms on which the intertemporal reallocation of the lifetime earnings stream can be effected. This, of course, assumes perfect capital markets and perfect foresight concerning future income streams. That is, frictionless intertemporal allocation requires that agents be able to borrow an amount equal to the lifetime earnings stream discounted at the appropriate interest rate.[5]

The predictions derived from the intertemporal optimization approach appear to be at odds with observed facts. For instance, the theory would predict an increase in aggregate savings rates in response to a change in the interest rate. Empirical studies of the determinants of household saving in general indicate that changes in interest rates exert a negligible impact on the level of aggregate saving.[6] Moreover, it is well known that countries with the highest rates of savings measured as a percent of disposable income historically tend to have had comparatively low domestic interest rates.

Of course, the microtheoretic approach to the consumption function points out the problems inherent in inferring macroeconomic behavioral relationships from an optimization problem of a "representative" agent. The foregoing prediction that agents, given stable preference functions, would choose to save more at every level of income given an increase in the interest rate does not mean that aggregate savings per time period would increase. In Keynesian theory the level of aggregate savings is a residual and is determined by national income and the propensity to consume. National income is determined by effective demand. If agents collectively prefer to save more at every level of income it will result in a contraction of effective demand, assuming no compensating increases in the other components of aggregate spending. This is the well known "Paradox of Thrift."[7]

This argument should not be taken to mean that interest rates are unimportant for household spending. However, interest rate movements seem more likely to influence the volume of consumer spending through the effect on the level of household borrowing. In an important sense, interest rates or finance charges on installment debt contracts are a part of the price of these items.[8] For example, a relatively small change in the interest rate charged on installment debt can have a major impact on the nominal amount of the periodic repayments stipulated in the contract. This is more likely to be the case where the good or service purchased represents a major outlay for the household. If we hold income, the average prices of goods and services, and tastes and preferences constant, economic theory would predict an inverse relationship between borrowing, and hence consumer spending, and the interest rate as a special case of the law of demand. Mankiw (1985) empirically examined the importance of real, as opposed to money, interest rates in the consumption function using U.S. quarterly data for the years 1950-1981.[9] What is the rationale for specifying real interest rates as the appropriate explanatory variable? In the theory of consumer behavior the assumption of "rationality" means that agent's supply and demand functions depend only on real magnitudes. In technical terms, supply and demand functions are homogeneous of degree zero in prices. Mankiw measured the interest sensitivity of consumer expenditure for nondurables and services and found that spending for durables was far more sensitive to changes in the real interest rate than was spending for nondurables and services. Mankiw inferred on the basis of these findings that agents substitute different categories of expenditure in response to relative price changes resulting from fluctuating real interest rates. The implication is that monetary shocks which impinge on real interest rates can influence the allocation of purchasing power among durables and nondurables; however, monetary policy may not be able to change the absolute volume of household spending. This proposition is at odds with Mankiw's own findings. Specifically, if changing real interest rates merely change the composition of spending between durables and nondurables, the coefficient relating interest rates to nondurable sales should have a positive sign. In fact, spending for nondurables and services were found to be a negative function of real interest rates in the period studied. Another problem with Mankiw's work is that the real interest rates specified in the model are calculated ex post. From the standpoint of the debtor or creditor, there is no way of knowing a priori what the real interest rate on a particular debt instrument will be. The yield in real terms can only be known once all terms of the debt contact have been executed and one can compare the stream of payments denominated in money terms against movements in the general price level which occurred during the repayment period specified in the contract. Of course, this difficulty can be removed by invoking rational expectations, which is an assumption made by Mankiw.

It will be argued in Chapter 3 that nominal rates, or finance charges expressed in nominal terms, are in fact the relevant decision variable from the standpoint of both borrowers and lenders. Furthermore, it will be argued that the emphasis on *nominal* as opposed to real interest rates *is not* reflective of irrational behavior if the appropriate distinction is made between uncertainty and risk. However, the evidence seems to indicate that the volume of durable spending is not particularly sensitive to movements in *nominal* interest rates. Hamburger (1967), for example, specified reduced form consumption functions which were estimated using quarterly data for the period 1953-1964. Hamburger was able to generate explanatory power only when the interest rate variables entered the equations specified with very long lags.

Regressions performed by Cuthbertson (1981) for the United Kingdom indicate that interest rates can have powerful effects on durable sales under conditions of extreme tightness in consumer credit markets. Cuthbertson explained his findings in terms of the structural characteristics of the consumer credit industry, i.e., the supply side of these markets is oligopolistic in structure and, as a result, there is a considerable degree of stickiness with respect to finance charges. Changing conditions in financial markets will be reflected in finance charge adjustments only under conditions of excess demand. These findings are in contrast to the empirical work of Bean (1978) and Mean (1979) in which interest rates were found to be statistically insignificant explanatory variables in durable sales specifications tested for the U.K.

Though consumer durables and installment debt are not often thought of as being complementary goods, they are nonetheless purchased in something approximating fixed proportions. This fact is illustrated by a strong statistical correlation between durable goods sales and new extensions of consumer credit. The relationship between interest rates and durable spending can therefore be approached indirectly through estimation of the interest elasticity of the demand for credit function.

The interest inelasticity of demand for consumer credit has often been assumed and has important policy implications. Paul F. Smith has commented:

> The assumption of the inelasticity of the demand for consumer credit has become a working tool of both theory and

> policy. It plays an important part in the justification for legal ceilings that are designed to assure the consumer that he is paying a "fair" price in relation to costs. In the field of monetary policy, the assumption of inelasticity of demand has become a fundamental part of the argument for selective controls on consumer credit.[10]

Furthermore, the fact that interest rates charged on credit card debt or installment loans are typically higher than those charged on commercial and industrial loans lends support to the argument the demand for consumer credit is inelastic. There are three possible explanations, however, for this phenomena. First, consumer loans on average might tend to be riskier than other types of loans and as such lenders attach a risk premium to these loans. On this point the evidence is unclear.[11] Another possibility is that administrative or other overhead costs might be larger on average for consumer loans than other types of loans. The third explanation is that financial institutions discriminate against household borrowers, i.e., the demand for credit by household is less sensitive to movements in the interest rate than is the demand for credit by firms. The inelasticity of the demand for consumer credit with respect to finance charges gives rise to an opportunity for third degree price discrimination on the part of financial institutions. Of course, the viability of this practice would depend on the lender's ability to discriminate among classes of borrowers based on differential willingness to pay. It will be argued in Chapter 4 that the nature of the financial services industry is such that segregation of borrowers based on willingness to pay *is* practicable.

The work of Juster and Shay (1964) generally supports the conclusion that the demand for consumer credit is interest inelastic. These findings have, however, been criticized because they attempted to derive empirical demand functions for different categories of loans which are in fact highly differentiated.[12] That is to say that even within the category of consumer loans there are often substantive differences which are not reflected by differing interest rates charged. These include collateralization requirements, minimum downpayment, term to maturity, and rebates.

The simplest approach has been to infer the inelasticity of the demand for credit on the basis of the spread between interest rates on consumer loans and rates on other types of loans. Those using this approach include Johnson (1961) and Mars (1965). This method tends to discount alternative explanations such as differences in lender's risk or lender's cost.

Smith employed a different technique and arrived at a different conclusion. Specifically, Smith argued that since most states have legal ceilings on consumer finance charges, financial institutions which were in fact practicing price discrimination would almost always charge the ceiling rate permitted under state usury laws. Regressions performed by Smith, however, indicate that there is no strong correlation between legal ceilings on finance charges and rates charged on bank loans. However, just because lending institutions are not charging the maximum rate allowed under state usury ceilings does not mean that these institutions are not practicing price discrimination. On the contrary, it could simply mean that the maximum permissible rate allowed on consumer loans does not happen to be that rate which, in the estimation of lending institutions, will maximize earnings on consumer lending operations.

This study is based on the proposition that monetary forces are significant in a treatment of the consumption function largely to the extent that the volume of consumer durable spending is crucially dependent on the willingness of households to engage in debt-financed spending and to the extent there are organizations which provide a regularized flow of consumer credit extensions. Certainly interest rates are not unimportant in this context; however, the literature on the interest rate-consumption linkage is deficient in several respects. While there has been considerable emphasis placed on the issue of the interest elasticity of the credit demand schedule, writers have paid insufficient attention to the problem of pricing in installment credit markets. Of particular interest is the relationship between changes in yields carried by short-dated financial assets, changing conditions in installment credit markets, and the volume of consumer durable spending. Understanding the mechanics of this relationship should shed light on the way in which policy initiatives of the central bank are transmitted to household spending behavior.

2.2 NET WEALTH EFFECTS

If net wealth enters as a determinant of consumption there exists another channel through which monetary shocks could affect household spending. If an initiative by the monetary authority were successful in changing the real value of net wealth held by the community, monetary policy would, in effect, shift the consumption function. This is illustrated by the following simple example, in which a number of the assumptions common in recent macroeconomic literature are made. Suppose that net wealth of the private sector consists of claims to income streams from real capital and "outside" money, i.e., money issued by the central bank.[13] The public sector engages in deficit finance through the issue of securities which are held by both the public and the central bank. The central bank retains exclusive rights to note issue, i.e., there is no "inside" money. Government securities do not constitute net wealth in so far as economic agents completely discount these assets in anticipation of a future tax liability.[14] Suppose the central bank elects to change the monetary base by purchasing securities from the general public. These securities are paid for with newly created money. Individual portfolios now consist of more money and fewer bonds. The change in the quantity of high-powered money in effect augmented the net wealth of the private sector. If the marginal propensity to consume out of net wealth exceeds zero, spending will increase.

The net wealth interpretation of the role of money in the consumption function has some interesting implications for the integration of Keynesian income-determination theory and general equilibrium analysis. The specific analytical apparatus used for this case is the IS-LM model. The equilibrium loci in the real and monetary sectors, respectively, are derived under conditions of complete independence of the goods and monetary spheres, meaning the equilibrium loci in the monetary sphere could shift with no resultant shift of the IS loci. However, the net wealth effect rules out the dichotomization of the macroeconomy into independent goods and monetary spheres. Movement along a single IS curve means that all factors which enter as determinants of the consumption function are held constant with the exception of income. However, unless the IS intersects the LM in a range where the LM is perfectly horizontal (the liquidity trap), it can be shown that every shift of the LM will induce a shift of the IS in the same direction. The magnitude of the shift depends on the sensitivity of consumption expenditure to changes in net wealth and the interest rate, a change in the equilibrium interest rate must induce a shift of the consumption function, meaning there will be a change in the average propensity to consume at every level of income. This must be true unless the marginal propensity to consume out of net wealth is equal to zero. So long as a shift in the LM puts pressure on the equilibrium interest rate, the IS curve must shift with every shift of the LM by virtue of the net wealth effect.[15]

Keynes unequivocally recognized the interest-induced net wealth effect. In Chapter 8 of *The General Theory* concerning the objective factors governing the propensity to consume, Keynes writes:

> Perhaps the most important, operating through changes in the rate of interest, on the readiness to spend out of a given income (i.e., the propensity to consume), depends on the effect of these changes on the appreciation or depreciation in the price of securities and other assets. For if a man is enjoying a windfall increment in the value of his capital, it is natural that his motives toward current spending should be strengthened, even though in terms of income his capital is worth no more than before; and weakened if he is suffering a capital loss.[16]

Patinkin's general equilibrium model of a monetary economy gives rise to a different interpretation of open market operations in the case where government bonds do in fact constitute net wealth of the private sector.[17] Patinkin demonstrates that real interest rates cannot remain invariant to monetary shocks if bonds are not fully discounted in anticipation of future tax liabilities. This phenomena is referred to as the "net-real-financial asset" effect.[18] Interestingly, open market operations can be nonneutral with respect to real interest rates in the Patinkin model even if government bonds do not constitute net wealth. Such a result can occur if there are "distribution effects," i.e., if capital gains and losses realized on government debt act to redistribute wealth to economic agents with differing marginal propensities to consume out of net wealth.

A wealth-affected consumption sector also plays a vital role in the transmission of monetary variables to the general level of economic activity in the Federal Reserve-MIT-Penn (FMP) model. Specifically, changes in monetary variables such as bank reserves or borrowed reserves translate to changes in spending via a "stock-price" effect. Modigliani estimates the marginal propensity to consume out of net worth to be .053.[19] Monetary variables affect net worth primarily through the influence of monetary policy on the market value of corporate equity. If stocks and short term bills are reasonable close substitutes in the view of wealth holders,[20] monetary shocks which alter the yields of short term instruments should "shift" the demand schedule for stocks with consequent impact on the market valuation of corporate equity.[21] Equations built into the FMP model predict that roughly one-half of the total change in economic activity resulting from a change in the money supply is accounted for by household spending induced by changes in net wealth. It is emphasized that movements in monetary aggregates are manifest in changes in household spending exclusively through the "stock-price" effect in the FMP model. Presumably the value of illiquid assets such as real estate or land remain invariant to monetary shocks.[22] Though the net wealth variable generates good explanatory power in the FMP model, a basic question arises: If fluctuations in the market value of corporate equity induce a shift of the consumption function, what part of the shift is due purely to a change in household wealth on the one hand and what part of the shift is related to "expectation" effects?

A frequent criticism of the Modigliani formulation is that the "stock-price" effect is in reality a proxy for the state of consumer confidence.[23] It is argued that because the stock market has proven to be a reasonably accurate predictor of the future course of corporate earnings and in so far as information concerning movements in market averages is regularly disseminated, the value of leading market indices constitutes an important piece of data on which expectations are conditioned.[24]

Woglom (1981) sought to empirically determine the relative importance of stocks as a component of net wealth and the role of stocks as implicit measures of consumer sentiment. Woglom concluded that stocks should not enter as an argument in the consumption function except as a proxy, albeit a poor one, for consumer sentiment. The "stock-price" interpretation of the transmission mechanism suggests that the power of the monetary authority to influence the general level of business activity would be greatly enhanced if open market operations were not restricted to the purchase and sale of government securities but could be extended to include the purchase and sale of corporate equity.

Mishkin (1976) contends that the degree of liquidity which characterizes the portfolio of household assets is more important than net wealth of the household sector considered by itself. That is, if the household portfolio consists mainly of illiquid assets for which imperfect markets exist, the conversion of these assets to liquid purchasing power is likely to entail considerable capital loss. This factor acts as a deterrent to spending. Conversely, financial assets which are traded in highly organized markets and can be disposed of to raise cash with a minimum of transactions cost. Hence, the marginal propensity to consume out of net wealth depends on the degree of liquidity of household balance sheets. Monetary policy stimulates consumption expenditure via the impact on the degree of liquidity which characterizes the asset side of the household balance sheet.[25] Regressions performed by Mishkin generally support the liquidity hypothesis. Changes in the market value of financial assets produce powerful effects on spending for durable goods.[26]

Drawing on estimates of wealth in the U.S. economy made by Kendrick (1976), Laumus and Ram (1981) compared the statistical significance of two categories of wealth as determinants of the consumption function over the period 1929-1969.[27] Wealth was divided into human and nonhuman components, and it was found that changes in holdings of nonhuman wealth had a far greater impact on all categories of expenditure by consumers. These findings are consistent with the liquidity hypothesis of Mishkin if human wealth is regarded as inherently less liquid than nonhuman wealth.[28]

The fundamental criticism of the net wealth interpretation of the transmission mechanism is that the distribution of wealth in the U.S. economy is highly skewed. There are several formidable problems relating to the measurement of net wealth of the private sector; however, there is considerable evidence to support the claim that the distribution of aggregate wealth in the U.S. economy is much more uneven than is the distribution of income.[29] Smith and Franklin (1975) estimated that the top 1% of wealth holders controlled 27% of total wealth in 1772.[30] Projector and Weiss (1966) estimated that the top 6% of wealth holders accounted for 57% of total wealth in 1962 while the bottom 46% held only 2%. Moreover, it appears that the wealth distribution function is highly stable.[31] Estimates prepared by Lampman (1962) reveal that the share of wealth held by the top 1% of the population was 32% in 1922 and decreased only slightly between 1922 and 1956. If wealth is highly concentrated among the top quintile of wealth holders, does it follow that the spending of households in the aggregate should be sensitive to changes in the real value of wealth holdings? Cross-sectional studies give ample evidence that the marginal propensity to consume out of disposable income is a declining function of the level of family income, at least beyond some threshold value. In view of the skewness of the wealth distribution function, and its apparent secular stability, changes in the market value of assets such as securities and equities are likely to affect only a small fraction of households which fall in the upper tail of the wealth distribution function. Thus, the net wealth linkage depends on the spending behavior of that segment of the population which is least likely to alter patterns of expenditure in response to fluctuations in income or wealth.

In contrast to the asset side of the national balance sheet, debt obligations are fairly evenly distributed across income and age groups. The Federal Reserve Board of Governors sponsored two surveys conducted by the Survey Research Center at the University of Michigan to address this issue. As part of the surveys, the share of total debt by each income quintile of the population was ascertained for the years 1970, 1977, and 1983. The data indicate that the middle three income quintiles account for the majority of debt outstanding in all three years.[32] The linkage of money to spending as operating through the price and availability of borrowed purchasing power, and the condition of household indebtedness, appears to be much more direct than the net wealth effect. The latter approach depends on an ambiguous term structure relationship and the sensitivity of the consumption function to changes in the market valuation of financial assets. Access to borrowed purchasing power and debt considerations are likely to affect the spending behavior of a much broader segment of households. A comprehensive treatment of the consumption function should not ignore these factors.

2.3 PORTFOLIO ADJUSTMENT EFFECTS

The transmission mechanism of money to real variables has also been modeled in a portfolio-theoretic framework. Tobin's portfolio balance approach to the demand for money is viewed in many quarters as a major theoretical advance from the Keynesian theory of liquidity preference.[33] Tobin's use of mean-variance analysis explicitly incorporates risk, and the benefits derived through portfolio diversification, as an explanation of why individuals would prefer to hold money when income-earning assets could be purchased. Moreover, Tobin's version of liquidity preference does not restrict the portfolio choice to money or bonds as is the case in the simple Keynesian formulation. As a general principle, we could say that the primary incentive to wealth accumulation is uncertainty with respect to the future course of economic events. Hence, individuals accumulate wealth in order to transfer purchasing power from the present into an uncertain future. It follows that assets which are held in portfolios must perform the store of value function, i.e., these assets must be effective vehicles for transferring purchasing power into the future. Money is an asset because it performs the store of value function. But what assets should be regarded as alternatives to money as a store of value? From the standpoint of empirics, this question could be satisfactorily dealt with through the measurement of the elasticity of substitution between a spectrum of assets which, at least in principle, are capable of performing the store of value function.

Modeling of the money-effective demand linkage in the context of portfolio theory obviously suggest that physical capital goods are substitutes for money in the estimation of portfolio holders. This point will be developed with reference to the work of Friedman and Tobin on the transmission mechanism.

In an important sense, Tobin's general equilibrium model of a monetary economy represents a theoretical refinement of the Keynesian interest rate-investment linkage.[34] But there is one significant point of contrast. In the pure Keynesian version, if the marginal efficiency of investment schedule is negatively sloped with respect to the interest rate, a monetary expansion which puts upward pressure on the price of bonds and downward pressure on bond yields can be expected to induce a change in investment spending the magnitude of which depends on the change in the interest rate and the interest elasticity of the investment demand schedule. Tobin's interpretation differs from the foregoing in that money does not stimulate investment spending directly through the effect on interest rates, but rather indirectly through the impact on Tobin's q. Tobin's q is defined as the ratio of the price of existing capital goods to the price of newly produced capital goods. Tobin assumes that there are highly developed secondary markets for capital goods such that agents should never experience any difficulty "getting out" of these assets. Since it is spending for newly produced capital goods which generates income to factors of production, an increase in the value of q will generate an increase in the volume of aggregate demand as portfolio holders substitute into newly produced capital goods as an optimizing response to a change in relative prices. It is important to note that Tobin's analysis of the transmission mechanism is firmly placed in the framework of the portfolio balance approach to the demand for money set forth in his oft-cited 1958 paper. The implication is that an open market purchase of securities by the central bank which results in an increase in the equilibrium value of q will stimulate aggregate demand as economic agents change the composition of wealth holdings in favor of newly produced capital goods.[35] Thus, Tobin's transmission mechanism depends on the assumption of gross substitutability. By gross substitutability we mean that assets such as physical capital goods are alternatives to money, bonds, or equities in the estimation of portfolio holders.

Though a grouping of Friedman and Tobin under the heading of "Portfolio Adjustment Effects" may strike the reader as odd, there are some important similarities in their respective approaches to the transmission mechanism. Friedman asserts that his version of the quantity theory conveys the flavor of the "Chicago Oral Tradition";[36] however, the theory set forth in the 1956 "restatement" paper owes more to the Keynesian theory of liquidity preference than to the quantity theory as espoused by Simons, Knight, *et al.*[37] Though Friedman is clearly in the neoclassical tradition with his emphasis on the transactions motive to liquidity, there is an implicit recognition of the store of value function performed by money.[38] The main point of contact between Friedman and Tobin is the assumption, albeit unstated, of gross substitutability. However, Friedman has taken the argument a step further by suggesting that consumer durable goods serve the store of value function and as such are an alternative to money, bonds, etc., in the portfolio.[39] Durable goods are viewed as one asset in a spectrum of assets which comprise the household portfolio, and as such, spending for durables is one way to carry purchasing power into an uncertain future, i.e., one way to store wealth. Whereas assets such as bonds or equities are trading in highly organized spot markets and carry on "explicit" yield, assets such as refrigerators, stereos, or home computers have an "implicit" yield. The implicit yield on, say, a refrigerator would be equal to the imputed economic value in real terms of the services yielded by the asset, e.g., making ice cubes or preventing spoilage, measured as a percent of the market value of the good. Other things being equal, an increase in the value of the existing stock of household durables will result in a change in the composition of household portfolios as agents substitute durables for other forms of wealth. The magnitude of the change depends on the elasticity of substitution between the types of assets held. A change in the nominal quantity of money creates a disequilibrium in the structure of asset holdings.[40] That is, an exogenous increase in the quantity of money in effect augments the liquid balances of agents and thus disturbs the desired relationship between the desired stock of real balances and the household estimate of permanent income. A disequilibrium in the structure of asset holdings is created by an increase in the quantity of money as agents find themselves with an excessive stock of liquid balances relative to other forms of wealth. To restore equilibrium, agents substitute into financial assets and consumer durables until the stock of liquid balances is drawn down to its "optimum" level, i.e., the stock of money balances, expressed in terms of goods, bears the desired relationship to the agent's calculation of permanent income.[41] Hence, monetary shocks can spill directly over into household spending via portfolio adjustment effects. Working with the Fisherine equation of exchange, and assuming the income velocity of money is roughly constant, the question is: If an increase in the quantity of money does stimulate spending for consumer durables (expressed in money terms), will the monetary shock result in an increase in the flow of physical output, an increase in the general price level, or some combination of the two? On this point, the monetarist position of the short run nonneutrality and the long run neutrality of money is well known.[42] Money can have real effects in the short run only if some agents (usually labor) suffer from "money illusion," or if the costs of adjusting contracts fixed in money terms is prohibitive.

The basic criticism of the portfolio-theoretic approach to the transmission mechanism concerns the assumption, usually implicit, of gross substitutability. The portfolio theoretic approach abstracts from the special properties of money which give rise to a speculative motive to liquidity. Physical capital goods and household durables are very poorly suited to perform the store of value function in a world of uncertainty. These goods often have the properties of indivisibility and heterogeneity. Moreover, spot markets for durables and capital goods often do not exist, and when they do exist they are in general very poorly organized.

In comparison, financial assets such as bonds or equities are traded in highly organized markets with specialist traders acting as residual buyers and sellers. Hence, there is a very high degree of uncertainty with respect to the future spot price of capital goods and consumer durables. Capital goods are purchased in order to gain access to an expected income stream which derives from their use in the production of goods and services. It is true that if the income stream net of running expense derived from investment in capital goods were known with complete certainty, the assumption of gross substitutability would be tenable. However, given the uncertainty attached to projections of future income streams and the fact that secondary markets are poorly developed, investment in capital goods constitutes a commitment which in many cases is irreversible. It follows that the liquidity premium carried by capital goods is negligible if not zero.

The same principles apply to household durable goods. Durable goods are held primarily because of the stream of services which derives from their use, not as a means of transferring purchasing power from the present to some future date, and not as a means of deferring economic decision making. Durable goods *are not* close substitutes for money and financial assets as a store of value. Therefore, the linkage of money to effective demand does not take place through the portfolio adjustments of wealth holding agents to monetary shocks. In fact, the portfolio theoretic approach is seriously misleading when considering the relationship between money and consumer spending in as much as the decision of the household with regard to the desired composition of the portfolio of financial assets is for, the most part, divorced from the decision to spend for newly produced consumer goods. Hence the set of considerations which figure into the former decision will most likely omit several factors which are very important in shaping the latter.

Among these are the attitude of the household toward debt obligations and the access of the household to consumer finance.

2.4 CREDIT AVAILABILITY EFFECTS

Section 2.2 reviewed literature dealing with the relationship between interest rates and consumer spending. Microtheoretic approaches typically incorporate the assumption of "perfect" markets in the sense of fluid movements of market prices toward equilibrium values. With the interest rate treated as one price in an n x 1 vector of prices facing agents, it follows that the "perfect market" hypothesis rules out the possibility of pervasive quantity-rationing in markets for consumer finance. However, as is discussed in detail in Chapter 4, the perfect market assumption is particularly inappropriate to the modeling of markets for consumer installment credit. There is some literature which deals with the problem of the "availability" of consumer credit and its effects on the volume of consumer spending. This section will review this literature.

It was previously stated that while consumer durables and consumer credit are not usually thought of as complementary goods, there is a strong statistical correlation between durable goods sales and new extensions of consumer credit. This is not surprising in so far as consumer credit has no value except that it facilitates the purchase of goods and services. It follows that any factor which is capable of exerting an influence over the price or availability of borrowed purchasing power will exert pressure on the volume of durable spending by virtue of a negative cross-price elasticity relationship. In principle, monetary policy could affect the price or availability of credit directly through selective controls on hire-purchase terms stipulated in installment debt contracts or restrictions on the composition of bank portfolios, or indirectly, by the use of the instruments of monetary control to manipulate member bank reserve accounts.[43] There is evidence to suggest that direct controls are important in determining the volume of durable spending in the United Kingdom.[44] Ball and Drake (1963) investigated the importance of direct regulation of hire-purchase terms for durable spending n the U.K. during the period 1957-III to 1961-IV. Ball and Drake concluded that changes in hire-purchase terms were a significant factor in explaining the volatility of durable sales in the period under study.[45] Allard (1979) constructed a hire-purchase credit variable which was then specified as an independent variable in consumer durable equations tested for the U.K.[46] Allard's work generally supports the findings of Ball and Drake. However, one result of Allard's work is that it takes a considerable period of time for a change in hire-purchase terms to be reflected in a change in the volume of durable spending.

Hamburger and Zwick (1977) used a stock adjustment model to assess empirically the effect of direct credit controls imposed in the United States in the years 1948-1952. They concluded that direct controls had a quantitatively trivial impact on expenditures for durable goods during the period of the study. These findings are in direct contrast to the findings of Maris (1981), who employed Sims-type causality testing to determine if selective controls (such as were tried during the Carter Administration) are effective in stimulating or attenuating durable sales.[47] Maris found that although causation is not unidirectional, i.e., part of the variation in hire-purchase terms can be explained by variations in durable spending, selective credit controls do exhibit a correlation with a decline in durable goods sales.[48]

A difficult and controversial issue concerns the impact of general credit restraint on the supply schedule facing households in financial markets. Part of the difficulty relates to discerning changes in the FED policy regime. For instance, there exists no device comparable to the full employment budget which would allow a researcher to detect periodic switches in the conduct of monetary policy. Consequently, researchers have sometimes inferred policy transitions from "tight" to "easy" money, or vice versa, on the basis of the behavior of some monetary aggregate such as M1, etc.[49]

Such is the approach used by Peterson (1976). Based on the behavior of M2, Peterson designated 1966-I to 1966-IV, 1968-I to 1970-II, and 1973-I to 1974-IV as periods of restrictive monetary policy. Peterson then reviewed the quarterly "Bank Lending Practice" surveys reported annually in the *Federal Reserve Bulletin* to determine if, in fact, senior loan officers were "less willing" to make installment loans during contractionary monetary phases than they would be otherwise. The evidence indicates that during the decade 1965-1974 the supply of commercial bank consumer credit was significantly reduced in the periods that Peterson arbitrarily designated as "contractionary." Evans and Kisselgoff (1968) reached the opposite conclusion:

> Available evidence indicates that, historically, the supply of funds to installment credit institutions and final users has been very elastic. This has made it possible to meet consumer demand for installment credit without a tightening of terms. A major factor responsible for such favorable supply conditions has been relatively high interest rates consumers have paid for this credit. Fluctuations in the volume of credit seem to have been caused by changes in demand rather than supply.[50]

Chapter 6 considers the effect of direct and indirect credit controls in the 1979-1982 recession, a period during which monetary policy was widely perceived to have been "contractionary."

2.5 SUMMARY

Chapter 2 has reviewed the literature pertaining to the linkage of money to consumption expenditure. This literature was grouped under four headings: (1) Interest rate effects; (2) Net wealth effects; (3) Portfolio adjustment effects, and; (4) Credit availability effects.

It was stated in Chapter 1 that monetary factors are important in a theory of the consumption function. Monetary factors enter as determinants of the volume of consumption expenditure largely because a significant proportion of total consumer expenditure is debt-financed. Thus the volume of consumer durable spending depends on the willingness of households to incur installment debt liabilities as well as the ability and/or willingness of commercial banks, finance companies, savings and loans, credit unions, and retailers to accommodate the demand for installment credit by the household sector. The literature concerning the transmission mechanism of money to consumer spending is deficient mainly because it does not deal with the problem of the factors which condition the household attitude toward debt. Nor does it consider in a comprehensive fashion the set of factors which determine the price and availability of installment credit. These questions form the central focus of Chapters 3 and 4.

NOTES

1. Friedman argues the Federal Reserve can peg nominal rates but not real rates, any change in money rates being offset by a money-induced change in the general price level. See Friedman (1968), p. 14.

2. For a cogent description of this process, see Robinson (1978), Chapter 6.

3. Keynesian economics is often deemed "unscientific" by contemporary macroeconomic theorists on grounds that it lacks appropriate microeconomic foundations. For instance, Lucas (1975) and McCallum (1987) argue that the Keynesian consumption function is theoretically defective because the "fundamental psychological law" upon which it is based applies directly to aggregate behavioral relationships, i.e., it is not derived from underlying microeconomic relationships.

4. The multiperiod objective function can be written as follows:

$$\sum_{i=1}^{n} \beta \mu(c_t)^{t-i}$$

where the representative agent has an n-period (not infinite) lifespan. $\beta = 1/1 - \delta$, where δ is the time preference parameter.

5. Intertemporal allocation problems pose the restriction that the sum of lifetime consumption expenditures cannot exceed the agent's initial endowment of wealth and the discounted present value of the lifetime earnings stream. However, this restriction is not binding if we allow for the possibility of bankruptcy.

6. See, for example, Friedman (1957), Ando and Modigliani (1963), and Duesenberry (1949).

7. See Keynes (1936), p. 84.

8. Finance charges on installment debt contracts or credit card extensions are classified as interest rates for our purposes. Spokespersons for the financial services industry typically reject this interpretation, citing high administrative overhead costs attendant to consumer lending operations as an explanation for finance charges. A more thorough discussion of this issue is deferred to Chapter 4.

9. In contrast to most empirical studies of consumer spending, Mankiw's approach does not involve statistical testing of a reduced form consumption function. Rather, Mankiw sets forth an intertemporal utility function to be optimized by a "representative" agent and then evaluates the first order (Euler) conditions necessary to achieve a maximum. This method was introduced by Hall (1978). Reduced form consumption functions are criticized on the grounds that they involve ad hoc specification of aggregate behavioral relations which are not deduced from a choice-theoretic optimization problem. Lucas has criticized the large scale econometric models built on income-expenditure principles (such as the FMP model) on these grounds. See Lucas, *op. cit*. Hall's method could not be used to test for the importance of non-price credit rationing because the Euler conditions cannot be realized in the absence of continuous market clearing in financial markets.

10. Smith (1985), p. 517.

11. Delinquency rates on various types of loans are published in *Business Conditions Digest*, Table IB. Based on a review of these series, it appears that there is no significant difference between delinquency rates on installment loans and delinquency rates on commercial and industrial loans. However, delinquency rates on credit card debt tend to be markedly higher than those on other installment loans. For a discussion, see Dessart and Kuylen (1986) and Connor and Cyrnak (1986).

12. See, for example, Greer (1975).

13. The distinction between "inside" and "outside" money was made by Gurley and Shaw (1960). Gurley and Shaw argue that "inside" money, or bank-created money is not a part of the net wealth of the private sector because it is a liability of the banking system. For a different view, see Pesek and Saving (1967), Chapter 4.

14. For a discussion of this issue, see Harris (1981), Chapter 3, and Barro (1974).

15. It can also be shown that the independence of monetary and real sectors does not hold in the case where a shift of the investment demand schedule generates additional requirements for finance at every interest rate. For a mathematical proof of this point, see Davidson, *op. cit*., pp. 175-179.

16. Keynes, *op. cit*., p. 94.

17. See Patinkin (1965). The effect of open market operations on real variables such as income and employment is not dealt with in the Patinkin model. Trading occurs within the Marshallian market period such that quantities or stocks cannot be adjusted in response to relative price movements during the process of tâtonnement. In effect, income and employment are exogenized by solving the equation for the labor market prior to the trading of nonlabor commodities.

18. This is analogous to the Pigouvian "real balance" effect when net worth is defined inclusive of government debt liabilities. It should be pointed out that the net wealth effect in Patinkin's model is a price-induced wealth effect as opposed to an interest rate-induced change in net wealth. See Patinkin, *ibid.*, p. 290.

19. Net worth is calculated by a weighted average of net worth over the previous year. For a description of the net wealth variable in the FMP model see Modigliani (1971).

20. The "Market Segmentation Hypothesis" holds that bonds and equities are in fact not close substitutes. Preferences regarding either type of wealth are formed on the basis of the attitude toward risk or specific requirements for income or capital certainty. For a discussion, see Makiel (1966).

21. To capture the relationship between short term interest rates and stock prices, Modigliani estimated a term structure equation. For a detailed description, see Modigliani, *op. cit.*, Appendix B.2.

22. For example, capital gains and losses on equities are included in the net wealth variable in the FMP model whereas changes in the market value of all other household assets and liabilities are excluded.

23. Fair (1971) criticized the FMP consumption function on this basis. Modigliani tested his specification for robustness by adding the MOOD index prepared by the University of Michigan center for Social Research as an explanatory variable. The estimates of the marginal propensity to consume out of net wealth continued to be statistically significant.

24. Changes in the value of market indices are weighted in the determination of the Index of Leading Economic Indicators. For a description, see Zarnowitz and Boschan (1975). For a discussion of the reliability of movements in market averages as predictors of the business cycle, see Bosworth (1975) and Kader (1985).

25. If monetary policy affects the price of financial assets in the economy, with no effect on the market value of illiquid assets held by agents, it follows that monetary initiatives will influence the degree of liquidity of the household portfolio. See Mishkin (1976), p. 642.

26. An important result of Mishkin's empirical work is that household indebtedness exerts a depressing influence on durable spending. The importance of debt variables in the consumption function is discussed in detail in Chapter 3.

27. Kendrick prepared annual data on the stock of human and nonhuman wealth in the U.S. for the period 1929-1969. A basic problem with Kendrick's methodology is that the wealth estimates are based on costs and not market values. See Kendrick (1976).

28. Friedman distinguished between human and nonhuman wealth. Human wealth is regarded as the least liquid form of wealth by Friedman since there is a limited market for human capital, and limitations regarding the substitution of nonhuman for human capital. See Friedman (1956), p. 253.

29. In principle, net wealth could be measured by summing the market value of household assets and subtracting liabilities. A basic problem is that highly organized markets do not exist for many types of assets that constitute net wealth of the private sector. Moreover, if data on the value of illiquid assets did exist, this would not necessarily reveal the underlying distribution of aggregate wealth. For discussion of these problems, see Goldsmith (1962), Kendrick, *op. cit.*, and Brittain (1978).

30. The estimates of Franklin and Smith omit wealth held in trust. This omission would lead to downward bias of the estimates if wealth held in trust were more tightly held than other forms of wealth.

31. Brittain investigated the importance of inheritances and bequests as determinants of wealth inequality, its stability, and perpetuation. See Brittain, *op. cit.*

32. Source: *Survey of Consumer Finances*. A large part of the growth of installment debt between 1970 and 1983 was accounted for households in the top income quintile. The top 20% of households by income level owed roughly 22% of debt outstanding in 1970 and 45.5% in 1983.

33. See Tobin (1958).

34. See Tobin (1969).

35. Tobin's G.E. model makes the restriction that all money is "outside" money; hence, open market operations have no effect on net wealth but only on the division of private sector portfolios between money, bonds, and physical capital, the three stores of value in the Tobin model. See Tobin, *ibid.*

36. Friedman, *op. cit.*, p. 249.

37. For a discussion of the Keynesian origins of Friedman's demand for money specification and the differences between the quantity theory of Friedman's predecessors at Chicago and the quantity theory *cum* Friedman, see Patinkin (1969), pp. 92-115.

38. This can be seen by the presence of rates of return on bonds and equities as arguments in Friedman's demand for money function. See Friedman, *op. cit.*, p. 255.

39. Perhaps the most explicit statement of the monetarist transmission mechanism is set forth in the 1963 paper of Friedman and Meiselman. Much of what follows is based on that paper.

40. Friedman argues that a change in the nominal quantity of money is exogeneously determined, i.e., determined by the Federal Reserve. The real quantity of money, i.e., the stock of liquid balances expressed in terms of goods, is determined "primarily" by the demand for money, which is taken as a stable function of the variables specified by Friedman. For a discussion of the exogeneity of the nominal money stock, see Friedman and Schwartz (1982), Chapter 3.

41. Friedman and Meiselman state that money has an "implicit" yield. An increase in the nominal quantity of money, *ceterus peribus*, presumably reduces the implicit yield on money and induces substitution into other forms of wealth by virtue of gross substitutability relations. The "implicit" yield is not, however, analogous to the Keynesian "liquidity premium" in so far as Friedman and Meiselman attribute a positive yield on money to its "convenience." See Friedman and Meiselman, *op. cit.*, p. 77.

42. See, for example, Friedman (1968), Gordon and Wilcox (1981), and Gordon (1982).

43. Direct policy would include regulations concerning the minimum or maximum interest rate or finance charge, the minimum downpayment, maximum length of contract, or controls on commercial bank holdings of consumer loans or loans to finance companies. Direct regulation of hire-purchase terms has been a frequent practice in he

U.K., but less so in the U.S. For a discussion, see Ball and Drake (1963).

44. The Bank of England maintained direct controls over the minimum downpayment and the maximum monthly repayment period until 1976 when controls were discontinued.

45. The findings of Ball and Drake have been widely criticized because the statistical estimates were based on a small sample size. Ball and Drake admitted that the short period of the study reduced confidence in the empirical results. See Ball and Drake, ibid.

46. Allard's measure is: HP = d = (1-d)/m, where d is the minimum percentage downpayment and m is the maximum monthly repayment period permitted by the Bank of England. Allard's measure is conceptually and operationally superior to any other proxy for credit conditions yet devised; however, direct regulation of hire-purchase terms has been an infrequent practice in the U.S. and as such good data on prevailing hire-purchase terms does not exist.

47. For a description of Sims causality testing, see Sims (1972).

48. Maris conjectures that policy makers react to an increase in the growth rate of household indebtedness by imposing credit controls; hence, causation is not unidirectional.

49. This approach gives rise to an additional problem. Namely, if we observe a change in the quantity of money, however defined, does it follow that the change is a direct result of FED policy initiatives? That is, is the nominal money stock determined exogenously or endogenously?

50. Evans and Kisselgoff (1968), p. 38.

Chapter 3

The Monetary Determinants of Consumption Expenditure

The argument was made in Chapter 1 that monetary factors are important in a theory of the consumption function primarily because a significant fraction of consumer expenditure is debt-financed. Thus the volume of consumer spending is partly dependent on the willingness of households to incur contractually enforceable installment debt obligations and partly dependent on the willingness and/or ability of commercial banks as well as nonbank financial intermediaries to accommodate the household demand for finance. To state the problem in familiar economic terminology, the volume of household borrowing which is produced by the interaction of supply and demand schedules in markets for consumer installment credit invariably exerts a powerful effect on the level of spending for consumer goods. Chapters 3 and 4 involve an extensive partial equilibrium analysis of markets for consumer credit. Chapter 3 focuses on the demand for consumer credit. Particular emphasis is placed on possible sources of instability in the household demand for finance.

As a preface to a detailed consideration of the factors which condition the household demand for finance, this chapter sets forth a theoretical argument concerning the appropriate budget constraint in credit money economies. Credit money economies are defined as economies in which bank liabilities serve as the primary medium of exchange and store of value. Section 3.1, "The Household Liquidity Constraint," is based on the following principle: In a credit money economy in which agents have access to finance, the relevant budget constraint is *not* given by the flow of disposable income per time period combined with the realizable value of household wealth holdings. Moreover, the neoclassical formulation of the budget constraint is not relevant in advanced credit money economies regardless of whether the constraint is posed for the individual agent or is intended to apply to economic agents at the aggregate level. It is argued in section 3.1 that the "hard" budget constraint of general equilibrium theory contains an implicit assumption concerning the role of financial intermediaries in general, and commercial banks in particular. A relaxation of this assumption has important implications for the appropriate budget constraint facing the household sector as well as the role of financial institutions in sustaining the level of effective demand.

Joan Robinson argued that the primary achievement of the Keynesian Revolution was to place the economic process in historical time with explicit incorporation of uncertainty, as conceptually distinct from actuarial risk, as a casual factor underlying exogenous shifts of the aggregate demand function.[1] Heretofore the problem of uncertainty or Keynesian "animal spirits" has been analyzed primarily as it affected the division by wealth-holding units of their portfolios between money, financial assets, and physical, producible assets.[2] It is argued in section 3.4 that a comprehensive treatment of the consumption function should *not* abstract from the element of uncertainty. The volume of aggregate consumption expenditure depends in part on the willingness of the household sector to enter into legally enforceable debt contracts. Installment debt contracts commit the household to a series of cash disbursements which typically extend into the future for a period of months or years. The ability of households to meet contractual cash flow obligations which come due at future dates cannot be predicted on the basis of actuarial principles. Uncertainty thus constitutes a destabilizing factor to the extent that it contributes to the psychological aversion of the household sector to debt obligations.

3.1 THE HOUSEHOLD LIQUIDITY CONSTRAINT

The proposition that "money matters" is widely accepted by contemporary practitioners of business cycle theory.[3] The issue in dispute concerns the precise nature of the interaction of the monetary sector and the real economy. A theory of the role of money in the consumption function is both irrelevant and inapplicable if one is attempting to analyze the behavior of a nonmonetary economy.

As a point of departure it is therefore necessary to describe the salient institutional features which distinguish nonmonetary from monetary economies. A basic difference pertains to the set of permissible exchange relations which prevail in nonmonetary and monetary economies, respectively. A hypothetical nonmonetary, or barter, economy as imagined by modern economists is one in which goods exchange directly for goods. In such economies money is a unit of account, but does not function as a generally acceptable medium of exchange. Nor is money "a subtle device for linking the present to the future," or a means to defer economic decision making in a world of uncertainty.[4] Money exists primarily to facilitate the dissemination of information to economic agents concerning relative prices of goods and services. Money is merely an accounting device and as such has no meaningful institutional content. The existence of money in nonmonetary economies has no significant impact with respect to the set of rules according to which economic activity proceeds. Money is neutral in the sense that a change in the quantity of money, or its rate of growth, has no impact on real variables such as output, employment, and economic growth.

The classic example of a nonmonetary economy is a Walrasian auction market. In such an economy, money is a numeraire or accounting device, i.e., one good in an n-good world. A particular good is singled out to perform the numeraire function, presumably because it possesses the properties of homogeneity and divisibility which make it an effective unit of account.[5] That is not to say that the commodity designated as the numeraire has no value, but rather its value does not in any way derive from its being generally acceptable in exchange. That is, money has no institutional properties which give it exchange value in terms of goods. Money is unambiguously neutral in nonmonetary economies.[6] An increase in the quantity of money will affect the exchange value of commodities expressed in terms of the numeraire, but *not* the exchange value of commodities expressed in terms of other commodities.[7] Money *cannot* augment the stock of real purchasing power in barter economies.[8]

Robert Clower has argued that the distinguishing feature of a monetary economy is that only money buys goods.[9] The institutionally permissible set of exchange relations precludes the possibility that goods exchange directly for goods and makes money ubiquitous to all exchanges. Thus, in monetary economies there is one thing which has value by virtue of its being generally acceptable in exchange. In the case, for example, that precious metals were used as money, then money might have some intrinsic commodity value apart from its being generally acceptable in exchange. However, in the case of fiat money, token money, or bank money where additions to the total stock of money require a negligible commitment of real resources, the value of money can be attributed solely to its institutional properties as money.

Having posed the restriction that "only money buys goods," it follows that economic agents desiring to obtain disposal over goods necessarily must possess money if their buying plans are to be realized. In neoclassical barter economies goods exchange directly for goods, i.e., all goods are money. Hence, spending by an individual agent is limited by the exchange value of the endowment of goods possessed by an agent. Moreover, the purchasing power of agents considered in the aggregate is constrained by the exchange value, expressed in terms of the numeraire, of the total endowment of goods possessed by all traders. This amounts to nothing more than a restatement of Walras Law.

In the case of a pure exchange economy where goods exchange directly for goods Walras Law is a tautology; however, this principle is both irrelevant and inapplicable in a monetary production economy. In fact, households and firms are constrained with respect to their actions in the economic sphere by the reservoir of liquid purchasing power at their disposal. If we accept as a basic premise that the rate of utilization of existing productive capacity is determined by the volume of aggregate expenditure per time period, a better way to approach the problem in the context of monetary theory is to study the principles which determine the availability of liquid purchasing power and the extent to which a given stock of liquid assets is disposed of to obtain command over goods. That is the essence of the approach taken here.

"Liquid purchasing power" is anything which is generally acceptable in exchange, i.e., anything which possesses the institutional properties of money. For something to be money it must be generally acceptable in the settlement of contractual obligations which are written in terms of money. Included among these are, of course, contractual debt obligations. To paraphrase Davidson, money is that thing which discharges contractual debt obligations.[10] What constitutes money in mature monetary economies? Clearly, government issued fiat or token money is liquid purchasing power. The general acceptability of government issued fiat money can be explained by the existence of legal institutions such as money contracts and contract enforcement as well as long established social convention. To the above we would add checkable deposits at credit unions, thrift institutions, and commercial banks. Davidson has summarized the conditions under which the liabilities of banks and other depository institutions become acceptable in exchange:

> Bank money is, of course, simple evidence of private debt contract, but the discovery of "clearing," that is the realization that forms of private debt can be used in the settlement of the overlapping myriad of private contracts immensely increased the efficiency of the monetary system. Three conditions are necessary in order for such a private debt to operate as a medium of exchange: (1) the private debt must be denominated in terms of the monetary unit; (2) a clearing institution for these private debts must be developed; and (3) assurances that uncleared debts are convertible at a known parity into the legally enforceable medium of exchange.[11]

Following Von Mises, bank transactions deposits are decomposed into two categories.[12] The first category is defined as "primary" deposits. Primary deposits are defined as liabilities of the commercial banks which are not offset on the asset side of the bank balance sheets by an income earning instrument, such as a promise to pay. When a primary deposit is created, the bank credits the depositor's account against the value of the cash received or against a check drawn by the depositor on another account either at the same bank or at another financial institution. In any case, the creation of the primary deposits does not result in a change of the quantity of money. Rather, a primary deposit comes into existence whenever there is a reallocation of the existing stock of purchasing power among economic agents.

A second category of bank money is defined as "derivative" deposits. A derivative deposit comes into existence whenever a commercial bank sells its liabilities in exchange for a promise to pay by the debtor. A derivative deposit is created when a bank monetizes a debtor's IOU. In the case of derivative deposits, the liabilities of the bank in the form of transaction deposits are matched on the asset side of bank balance sheets by a promise to pay. Keynes explicitly recognized the distinction between primary and derivative deposits:

> (Such) a bank creates claims against itself for the delivery of money, i.e., what, hereafter, we shall call Deposits, in two ways.

> In the first place it creates them in the shape of either case or of an order (i.e., a cheque) authorizing the transfer of a deposit in some bank (either another bank or itself). . . . But there is a second way in which a bank may create a claim against itself. It may purchase assets, i.e., add to its investments, and pay for them, in the first instance at least, by establishing a claim against itself. Or the bank may create a claim against itself in favor of a borrower, in return for his subsequent reimbursement; i.e., it may make loans or advances.[13]

It is through the monetization of IOUs, or what is the same thing, the creation of derivative deposits, that the commercial banking system is able to augment the stock of liquid purchasing power at a point in time. Moreover, a decline in deposit creation can be expected to result in a diminution of aggregate purchasing power. The fundamental connection between the activities of the commercial banking system and the behavior of real magnitudes therefore exists in the expansion or contraction of bank-created monetary claims on the part of financial institutions. This conclusion follows from the fact that the realization of spending plans by economic agents, both households and firms, in many cases is contingent upon access to finance; hence, the banking system takes on a vital role in facilitating the convergence of notional and effective demand functions. The term "notional" demand has a different meaning here from the meaning of the term in the context of Clower's "dual decision hypothesis." In Clower's model, notional and effective demand functions diverge whenever "realized current income is less than notional current income," i.e., agents face quantity constraints in labor or product markets.[14] By "notional" demand we mean those spending plans that agents *would* carry out in the absence of quantity constraints in credit markets as well as labor and product markets.

Some might argue that in fact we are confusing credit with money. The argument is apparently based on the notion that credit is something distinct and altogether different from money.[15] In this study the terms "money" and "bank credit" are used interchangeably. To have access to credit means to have access to a source of purchasing power which takes the form of a transaction deposit. Transaction deposits are money by virtue of their being generally acceptable in exchange.

When attempting to define those things which constitute "money" in advanced monetary economies, a problematic issue concerns the appropriate treatment of unused credit lines or overdraft facilities. When applying the "money is what money does" criteria, overdraft facilities are not usually regarded as money because they cannot be properly treated as a store of value. The firm which has been extended a credit line by a commercial bank has access to a stock of ready purchasing power, but the overdraft facility as such does not constitute an asset from the standpoint of the firm nor does it represent, technically speaking, a liability of the bank. However, this section is primarily concerned with the way in which the sources of liquid purchasing power place an upper limit on the volume of aggregate demand. In fact, the use of monetary aggregates such as M_1, etc., as proxies for the existing stock of ready purchasing power are very misleading in so far as unused credit lines are omitted from consideration. Though there is no statistically accurate data concerning the dollar amount of unused overdraft facilities, inclusion of unused overdrafts in the definition of monetary aggregates would undoubtedly increase the value of such aggregates as M_1 by a significant amount.[16] From the standpoint of the firm, the purchase of capital goods or hiring of factors of production can be effected through a drawdown on its existing account of transactions balances or through the use of overdraft permission granted by the banking system. Keynes commented on this phenomena in his *Treatise On Money*:

> We have characterized cash-deposits as furnishing the ready command over money which is required for convenient transaction of current payments. But the analysis is complicated, in a modern community by the fact that cash deposit is not the only means of providing this facility. It is provided, equally well, by the overdraft (in ital.). A customer of a bank may draw a cheque against his deposit, thus diminishing his credit (in ital.) with the bank: but he may, equally well, draw a cheque against his overdraft, thus increasing debit (in ital.) with the bank. It is just as effective to pay by increasing the debit balance of the creditor as it is by decreasing the credit balance of the former and increasing the credit balance of the latter.[17]

It might be argued that a discussion of the appropriate categorization of overdraft facilities is irrelevant in this context since we are concerned with modeling the determinants of household spending. However, a bank card extension to a household is in many ways similar to the granting of overdraft permission to firms. In both cases the debtor has the option of borrowing, without prior notice, an amount of funds up to some limit specified by the bank. Moreover, extensions of credit lines to households by retailers and commercial banks are very substantial. Unused credit card extensions therefore constitute a significant source of idle purchasing power and should not be ignored.

To recapitulate the argument set forth to this point, it was stated that a basic institutional feature of monetary economies is that money enters on one side of every bilateral exchange. Of course, there are exceptions to this principle, i.e., real world cases where goods exchange directly for goods. However, such exceptions can be safely ignored in that the vast majority of transactions involving newly produced goods and services entail an exchange of money for goods. The task now is to develop the implications of the "cash in advance" proviso with respect to both the relevant constraints on household spending and the relationship between the activities of the commercial banking system and the level of effective demand.

It is a truism that consumption expenditure per time period cannot exceed the aggregate purchasing power of the household sector. Thus, a theory of the consumption function begins with a delineation of the sources of household purchasing power. The primary source of household purchasing power is obviously the flow of current income received by households. Wages and salaries, profits and dividends, rental and proprietor's income accrue to economic agents in the form of money as opposed to goods and as such constitutes liquid purchasing power. Given the fact that income represents the major source of household purchasing power, changes in the flow of income per time period can be expected to exert the dominant influence on the volume of consumption expenditure in any given time interval. In the naive Keynesian formulation, the fundamental psychological law gives rise to a stable relationship between consumption expenditure and the flow of income accruing to households.[18] Consumption expenditure is a magnitude which is passive or determined by other variables in the system. Hence, the instability of the aggregate demand schedule cannot be explained in a plausible way on the basis of sudden exogenous shifts of the consumption function. Indeed, the inherent stability of the consumption function has been generally accepted by mainstream adherents to Keynesian theory.[19] Hyman Minsky has summarized this view as follows:

> In the *General Theory* the consumption-function construct serves the purpose of identifying the passive, or determined, component of aggregate demand: in no sense is the consumption function "the heart of macroeconomics," if modern macroeconomics is identified with Keynes. In Keynes view it is, if an anatomical analogy is necessary, the passive skeleton of macroeconomics which nevertheless conditions the system's responses to stimuli.[20]

A second source of household purchasing power is the stock of household wealth, or to be more specific, the realizable or liquid value of the stock of household assets. As was pointed out in Chapter 2, Keynes recognized that the market revaluation of financial assets could exert an influence on the propensity to consume out of a given flow of income. This principle was defined as the interest rate-induced net wealth effect. When evaluating the effect of changes in the value household wealth on the average propensity to consume at every level of income, two factors must be taken into consideration.

First, since we are concerned with the determination of *aggregate* consumption expenditure, a factor of decisive importance is the distribution of wealth among various income or wealth holding groups in the economy. Conceptually, we could construct a Lorenz curve depicting the distribution of wealth in a particular economy. Using data taken from the Lorenz curve, a Gini coefficient is calculated.[21] As a general principle we state the following: *Ceteris peribus*, as the Gini coefficient moves toward a value of zero, the greater the sensitivity of aggregate consumption expenditure to changes in the market value of household wealth. That is to say that the more even the distribution of wealth across the population, the greater the impact on spending resulting from a given change in the market value of assets held by households. Conversely, the more uneven the distribution in the economy, the smaller the impact on spending resulting from a market revaluation of household assets. The principle could be interpreted as a corollary to the fundamental psychological law. In the case where the existing stock of wealth is very tightly held, changes in the market value of household assets can be expected to impinge on the spending decisions of a very small percentage of households. The principle stated above is admittedly an inductive judgment lacking of empirical verification. However, there is little doubt that the distribution of wealth in the U.S. economy *is* highly skewed in favor of the top quintile of wealth holders.[22]

With respect to the importance of wealth in the consumption function, a second consideration is the degree of liquidity which characterizes the asset side of the household balance sheet. That is, the decision by an agent to effect a drawdown on the stock of assets possessed to finance desired consumption expenditure depends in part on the relative ease or difficulty in converting these assets into money. In the case of where the portfolio consists mainly of financial assets which are traded in highly organized markets, the issue is fairly clear cut, i.e., a sudden change in the real value of these assets is likely to induce a shift of the consumption function. However, for a broad segment of households, wealth is concentrated in illiquid assets such as home equity and household durables. Given the lack of organization and "thinness" of secondary markets for durable goods, it is often likely to be true that the subjective (imputed) economic value of the services yielded by a particular illiquid asset will exceed its realizable value in exchange. The sale of durable goods is likely to entail both considerable search costs and the potential for capital loss. Hence, there are strong disincentives attached to a drawdown of illiquid assets for the purpose of raising purchasing power, and such a drawdown may in many cases be associated with a "distress" sale.[23]

To income and wealth we add a third source of purchasing power, namely, borrowing or credit. It was stated in Chapter 1 that the primary function of financial institutions consists in the creation and sale of monetary claims which give debtors command over goods. If financial institutions are willing to create a demand deposit in exchange for a promise to pay by a particular customer, then this consumer has a stock of purchasing power at his disposal which, for the moment at least, exceeds the sum of wealth derived from his stock of wealth (inclusive of human wealth) at the market value of his wealth holdings. Moreover, if an economic agent has continued access to credit, spending could theoretically exceed the value of income and wealth for an indefinite period of time. If a financial institution is continually willing to monetize the IOUs of a particular agent, this agent could in principle "live beyond his means" in perpetuity. Recognition that households do in fact have considerable access to borrowed purchasing power has important implications for the relevant constraints facing a single household or households considered in aggregate. Spending cannot exceed purchasing power; however, in an economy characterized by increasing access of households to markets for consumer credit, the sources of purchasing power are not restricted to the sum of current income received by households or the liquid value of household wealth. Given this fact it is more logical to treat the household as facing a *liquidity* constraint as opposed to an income or wealth constraint. It follows that the effect of increasing participation of commercial banks and nonbank financial institutions is a relaxation of the liquidity constraints facing households. Table 3-1 shows extensions of consumer credit by financial institutions in selected postwar years. Note in the time period 1955-1980 extensions of consumer credit in real terms increased by 271%. Hence, the growth rate of new extensions of consumer credit, as well as the growth rate of debt outstanding, exceeded the growth rate of real disposable income in every decade since World War II.

Table 3-1

Extensions of Consumer Installment Credit by All Suppliers and Per Capita Personal Disposal Income in Selected Years (in 1982 Dollars)

Year	Extensions Of Installments Credit (in billions)	Percent Change	Per Capita Disposable Income	Percent Change
1955	$137.2	--	$5,712	--
1960	162.9	+18.7	6.036	+5.7
1965	222.6	+36.6	7,026	+16.4
1970	248.4	+11.6	8,133	+15.6
1975	286.2	+15.3	8,944	+10.0
1980	373.0	+30.3	9,722	+8.6

Source: *Federal Reserve Bulletin* and *Business Conditions Digest.*

The data clearly indicate that, abstracting from cyclical disturbances, a secularly increasing proportion of total consumption expenditure is financed through household borrowing. In fact in 1982 roughly one-third of total consumer spending was financed through borrowing.[24]

On a purely theoretical level it might be argued that the flow of income and the liquid value of the stock of household assets do in fact place an upper limit on the physical quantity of goods and services which could be purchased in a given period of time. That is, it is necessary to distinguish between constraints on purchasing power for an agent considered individually and the budget constraint relevant to the economy as a whole. A simple example will illustrate this point. Consider an economy in which, at time t, there are no accumulated stocks of wealth other than in human wealth. Highly developed markets exist for borrowing and lending such that agents may effectively reallocate the lifetime earnings stream (which is assumed to be known with complete certainty) and thus optimize an intertemporal objective function. Suppose that for a particular group of agents the structure of preferences is such that current consumption is more highly valued than consumption in future periods. Utility maximization necessarily requires that a fraction of future earning be discounted at prevailing interest rates. That is to say agents must borrow. To the extent that financial intermediaries merely act as conduits to facilitate the reallocation of *existing* purchasing power among agents with differing rates of time preference, dissaving by one set of agents necessarily requires an act of volitional saving by at least one other agent. That is, the substitution of current for future consumption can be accomplished only if at least one agent is willing to defer spending in the current period. Such a scenario is consistent with the classical interpretation of Say's Law and the Marshallian conception of the interest rate as the "reward for waiting."[25]

If we divide the economic process into discrete time intervals it is true by identity that the sum of spending is equal to income in each time interval. It follows that aggregate spending per time period *cannot* exceed the flow of income per time period. However, can it be inferred on the basis of accounting identities that aggregate demand is *constrained* absolutely by the flow of income generated by the production and sale of goods and services? Such a conclusion, though it calls into question the legitimacy of the liquidity constraint as a useful or realistic concept with respect to the modeling of aggregate phenomena, is based on an incomplete view of the nature of modern banking institutions. Financial intermediaries do not merely act as agents to transfer purchasing power from savers to borrowers but are actively engaged in the creation of liquid purchasing power. The restriction that saving and borrowing net out to zero in each time interval is clearly inappropriate for advanced monetary economies. Moreover, the fact that banks create purchasing power when they monetize the IOUs of debtors *does not* mean that spending will exceed income in any time interval. The increase in borrowing which is, by accounting principles, spent only to create additional income (the other side of the double entry) merely means that, in the context of national income accounting, the equality of saving and investment does not constitute a constraint on aggregate spending. This can be seen as follows. Suppose that, other things being equal, the banking system creates a given sum of transactions deposits on behalf of a certain debtor. The debtor then purchases a newly produced consumer item through a drawdown on his transactions deposit. The money spent for the purchase of the consumer good obviously accrues to someone as income, yet the purchasing power required to effect the transaction did not derive from the production and sale of goods or services in the current period or in any past periods. Hence, the identity of spending and income holds even if it is allowed that banks create purchasing power which has no connection to the current or past production and sale of goods and services. It follows that aggregate demand *is not* constrained by income in mature monetary economies.

If we are describing an economy in which households either have no access to credit or exhibit a strong psychological aversion to incurring debt liabilities, the passive or stable behavior of the consumption function would be a tenable proposition. Spending would depend almost entirely on income and short run fluctuations in household spending could likely be explained almost entirely in terms of short run movements in income. However, institutional changes in the postwar era call into question the accuracy of this interpretation. That is to say, we are clearly dealing with an economy in which households *do* have access to credit and exhibit a willingness to incur debt as a means to obtain disposal over goods. The cumulative effect of these institutional changes can be stated as follows: In comparison with an economy in which households do not borrow, if financial institutions do in fact create monetary claims on behalf of households a relatively greater proportion of total consumption expenditure will depend on factors *other than income*. The growth and proliferation of consumer financing arrangements therefore has the effect of eroding the connection between income and consumer spending.

In Chapter 3 of the *General Theory*, Keynes decomposed aggregate demand into two parts: That spending which depends on income (D_1) and that spending which does not depend directly on income (D_2).[26] The stable component of aggregate demand, i.e., consumption, Keynes put under the heading of D_1. This was a logical categorization in so far as Keynes was analyzing the unemployment problems of economies in which the volume of nonmortgage household borrowing was very small in comparison to the volume borrowing by firms.[27] Hence, one could safely abstract from the importance of monetary influences in the determination of consumer expenditure. Such an abstraction is, however, inappropriate in the case where a nontrivial fraction of consumption expenditure is financed with bank-created monetary claims. If we take into account the fact that households borrow extensively, it follows that at least some proportion of total consumption expenditure should logically be put under the heading of D_2, i.e., some fraction of household spending will not depend directly on income. This is not to say it is possible to make a neat division between that consumption expenditure which depends on income and that consumption expenditure which does not depend on income. Clearly, all categories of private spending depend in some way on the flow of current income, if only for the reason that projections of future income flows are likely to be conditioned by information concerning current income flows. However, it is possible to decompose consumption expenditure into that spending which is determined primarily by income and that spending which is determined primarily by factors other than income. It is first necessary to divide consumer spending into two categories: That part of spending which is endogenous, i.e., is primarily determined by income and therefore is essentially immune to monetary influences; and that spending which is exogenous and hence *is* sensitive to monetary influences. Spending for consumer nondurable goods and services falls into the first category. The second category includes spending for consumer durable goods. This is admittedly an imperfect taxonomy. Such a classification is based on the assumption that households incur nonmortgage debt primarily as a means to facilitate the purchase of durable goods. However, there is evidence indicating secular changes in the pattern of credit use. It appears that an increasing fraction of purchases of nondurables and services are financed through borrowing. This is particularly true in the case of credit card debt and home equity loans.[28]

Moreover, the trend toward the financing of nondurables and services through borrowing has been very pronounced in the recovery from the 1979-1982 recession. Nonetheless, installment borrowing in the postwar period represents the bulk of household nonmortgage borrowing and most installment debt is used to finance the purchase of big-ticket durable items such as automobiles, furniture and fixtures, and household appliances.

The durable series has been subject to numerous shocks such as changes in the rate of family formation, the cyclical nature of residential construction activity, product innovation, irregularly recurring replacement cycles, and bottlenecks created by strike activity to name a few. These factors are omitted from consideration here not because they are unimportant in explaining the short run instability of durable spending but rather because they do not bear directly on the problem at hand.

The demand for credit on the part of households is an expression of the demand for goods and services. That is, households incur debt as a means to obtain disposal over goods.[29] Thus, other things being equal, the volume of durable spending can be expected to fluctuate in direct proportion to the volume of new credit extensions to households. It is therefore important to delineate those variables which determine the extent to which households add to their debt liabilities.

3.2 FACTORS CONDITIONING THE HOUSEHOLD ATTITUDE TOWARD DEBT

The previous section decomposed the consumption function into endogenous and exogenous components. The endogenous component (defined as C_1) is that proportion of consumption expenditure which is determined primarily by the flow of current income. The exogenous component (defined as C_2) is that part of consumption expenditure which is determined by factors other than income. The thesis is concerned with explaining short run movements in this volume of consumer durable spending. In so far as durable spending was put under the heading of C_2, it now becomes important to specify and analyze the forces which interact to determine the volume of exogenous consumption expenditure. Exogenous consumption expenditure is taken to be a function of four determinants: (1) The price of consumer credit as expressed by the finance charge, interest rate, or annual percentage rate; (2) the price of durable goods; (3) the attitude of the household toward debt obligations; and (4) the access of the household sector to finance.[30] This section is concerned with the third determinant of exogenous spending, or more specifically, the complex of factors which condition the household attitude toward debt. Thus, the analysis which follows abstracts from the other three determinants of exogenous spending by assuming that households face perfectly elastic supply schedules in both credit and durable goods markets at prevailing hire-purchase terms and durable goods prices, respectively.[31]

The household attitude toward debt, as reflected in the volume of household borrowing and durable spending, is influenced by the following set of factors: (1) Prevailing social attitudes toward the use of consumer credit; (2) the size, quality, and age composition of the existing stock of durables owned by households, and; (3) the assessment by the household of its ability to make good on newly created cash flow commitments which result from installment borrowing.[32] The third factor is in turn specified to be a function of the following variables: (1) The level of current income as well as expected income flows in future periods; (2) the current status of the household balance sheet, or more specifically, the fraction of liquid asset holdings and/or current and anticipated income receipts which are expected to be claimed by the servicing of existing contractual cash flow commitments; and (3) tax provisions applying to the deductibility of interest charges or sales taxes incurred on durable goods purchases.

A factor of decisive importance in explaining the secular expansion of household credit use has been the general liberalization of prevailing social attitudes toward indebtedness or the development of habits of mind favorable to borrowing. In the early decades of the twentieth century there remained a widespread social stigma attached to household nonmortgage borrowing. Installment borrowing was frequently the subject of scathing editorials and satirical cartoons. The use of installment credit was typically regarded as a means to engage in extravagant spending or to "live beyond one's means." The practice of installment borrowing was viewed as being inconsistent with the values of thrift and sound finance. Moreover, the consumer credit business was held to be inherently exploitive of borrowers.[33]

The evolution of attitudes toward debt is fundamentally related to the technological revolution which established the automobile as the primary mode of transportation. No less important was the dramatic effect on urban land use patterns resulting from the massive infrastructure built to accommodate automobility. As a general observation, the emergence of the automobile and the construction of the modern infrastructure designed to facilitate auto access had the effect of increasing the average distance traveled to the workplace. Thus, participation in modern labor markets and social life generally requires that individuals have access to car transportation. But the outright purchase of a big ticket item such as a car more often than not creates a liquidity problem in the household. Hence the necessity of borrowing. Table 3-2 gives per capita installment debt in selected years as well as per capita installment debt collateralized by automobiles. The data clearly indicate that the secular increase in the demand for car loans is an important factor in explaining the dramatic increase in per capita household indebtedness (excluding mortgage debt). Given that there will typically be less aversion to borrowing if the consumer views the item financed as a necessity as opposed to a luxury, the relaxation of social attitudes toward credit use, and concomitant increase in indebtedness of the household sector, is strongly related to the changing status of the automobile from a luxury good to a necessity.

Table 3-2

Total Installment Credit and Automobile Credit Per Capita Outstanding in Selected Years (in 1982 Dollars)

Year	Total Per Capita Installment Credit Outstanding	Per Capita Automobile Paper Outstanding
1939	$ 246.47	$ 81.94
1950	317.34	131.28
1960	813.20	334.19
1970	1,270.15	465.95
1980	1,679.58	626.01
1985	2,085.62	811.42

Source: *Federal Reserve Bulletin*, and the *Statistical Abstract of the United States*.

Aside form the secular behavior of per capita indebtedness, prevailing social attitudes toward debt are revealed in terms on which households purchase credit as well as the types of goods and services financed through credit use. With respect to the first point, a key indicator would be the average length or maturity of installment debt contracts as compared to the useful life (as measured, say, in years) of the good or service financed through credit use. Do consumers behave conservatively in the financing of durable purchases, and what rules of thumb might be applied to determine if in fact the household practices "sound" finance? The financing of durable goods through installment debt contracts can be viewed as a form of sinking fund finance.[34] Davidson defines sinking fund finance as:

> [What] occurs when contractual debt obligations are written in money terms in a time sequence so that the expected quasi-rents earned by the asset and/or other unencumbered cash inflows expected by the holder exceeds contractually due interest on any amortization of principle in each period by a sufficient amount to at least provide for the redemption of the remaining debt principle at the maturity date.[35]

As was stated in Chapter 2, households do not as a regular practice take positions in consumer durables in anticipation of a stream of quasi-rents which is expected to derive from their use in roundabout production.[36]

Based on the criteria given above, and assuming that the useful life of new durable goods remains roughly constant over a period of years or decades, shifts in the nature of household borrowing practices from "sound" to "unsound" finance could be detected by secular changes in the average length of installment debt contracts. Under the direct credit controls in effect from 1948-1952, the maximum length of an installment debt contract was limited to 12 months. The average maturity of car loans quickly increased to 17 months with the introduction of the 24 month installment contract in 1953. The average maturity on installment car loans collateralized by autos increased to 45.5 months by 1980. In 1986 the average maturity of a car loan was 50 months.[37] The average maturity of a car loan increased by 26% between 1954 and 1980. Such a trend indicates that household on average have become progressively less conservative with regard to their borrowing practices.

This conclusion could be erroneous if, owing to technical improvements or better maintenance, the useful life of durable goods such as autos is longer in more recent years and decades as compared to earlier periods. It has been estimated that the median lifetime of a motor vehicle was 10.2 years in the period 1969-1978 and 10.9 years from 1979-1982.[38] This increase is probably more the result of the cyclical contraction of auto sales in the 1979-1982 recession than technical improvements or other factors. Domestic auto sales declined by approximately 13 billion dollars between 1979 and 1980. A decrease in auto sales will under ordinary circumstances be accompanied by a fall in scrappage rates as households postpone the purchase of a new car. Also, there is evidence to suggest that the median lifetime of a car has not changed much between 1945 and 1970 if the average age of a passenger car in use is any indication. Table 3-3 gives the average age of a passenger car in use in selected postwar years.

Though the data are not free of trend and cyclical influences, they give a good first approximation.[39]

Table 3-3

Average Age of a Passenger Car in Use in Selected Years

Year	Average Age of a Passenger Car in Use (Years)
1945	7.3
1950	7.8
1955	5.9
1960	5.9
1965	5.9
1970	5.5
1975	6.0
1980	6.6
1985	7.6

Source: Automobile Manufacturers Association.

Moreover, it is well known that heavy advertising as well as frequent design modifications in the automobile industry are directed towards stimulating replacement demand, or shortening the average duration of replacement cycles.[40] In summary, the evidence does not support the contention that maturities on installment debt contracts have lengthened to reflect an increase in the useful life of durable goods.

Does this mean that the current generation of households is less conservative with respect to its borrowing habits than proceeding generations? Not necessarily. Or at least not from the perspective of a representative household. Rather it is likely that consumers tend to make financing decisions on the basis of cash flow, as opposed to balance sheet, calculations. That is to say that the relevant consideration in most cases is not the amortized value of the physical stock of durables in relation to existing installment liabilities, but rather the portion of disposable income claimed by debt servicing per week, month, etc. This point becomes important when evaluating the impact of total installment debt liabilities to personal disposable income as the appropriate proxy of short-term pressure exerted on the budget constraint by household indebtedness.[41] However, assuming disposable income remains constant, it is possible for the percentage of monthly income claimed by debt servicing to remain constant even if the ratio of installment debt to income is increasing. Such a possibility arises if the average maturity of installment debt contracts (measured in months) increases by a sufficient amount.

The size, quality, and age composition of the existing stock of durables should influence the willingness to assume debt.[42] A few points need further discussion here. First, there is considerable ambiguity as to the effect of the size of the per capita stock of durables on the demand for household finance. Williams has described the problem as follows:

> Existing stock may influence current purchases in three ways: through saturation, demonstration (or habit) and replacement effects. The market saturation effect produces an inverse relationship between stocks and current purchases; the demonstration and replacement effects a direct relationship. In empirical work it is difficult to isolate each of these factors and often the coefficient of stock in a demand equation represents only the net effect.[43]

A finding that the demonstration effect dominates the saturation effect, i.e., the partial derivative of durable spending with respect to the per capita durable stock is positive, would be generally consistent with Veblen's theory of pecuniary emulation as well as Duesenberry's theory of the secular consumption function.[44]

That the introduction of new, innovative durable goods such as television sets, or more recently, home computers, produces powerful effects on the volume of durable spending is well known. In addition, durable goods such as autos, recreational vehicles, and appliances undergo continual quantitative changes which, whether they are of a cosmetic or technically substantive in nature, generally improve the incentive to sell or scrap existing durable goods.[45]

Numerous durable goods industries have enjoyed impressive growth following the introduction of an innovative and widely affordable product. However, there is a tendency as the industry matures for an increasing proportion of total sales to constitute replacement demand. This phase of the industry lifecycle, as it is sometimes referred to, is characterized by redundant capacity, the consolidation of rival firms, the rise to preeminence of a few dominant firms and the exit of others.[46] The development of the automotive and television industries seem to fit this general pattern. Such a phenomena may impart a degree of instability to the durable series by virtue of two effects. The first effect might be referred to as the "Schumpeterian groundswell" effect.[47] With regard to durable spending, the groundswell effect can be illustrated by a simple example. Suppose a new durable good with a useful life of three years were introduced. Assume the population remains constant with no births or deaths. In year one suppose 1/10 of the population purchases the new durable good. In year two 2/5 of the population buys the new product for the first time and in year 3 the remaining half of the population makes its first purchase. After three years every member of the population has purchased the new product and the industry has enjoyed impressive growth 3 years running. It is clear, however, that the industry will suffer a major slump in its fourth year because replacement demand will be sufficient to absorb *only* 70% of the units sold in the third year. Such an effect may well have been operative in the automotive industry between 1921 and 1933. For example, it has been estimated that 23% of new vehicle sales were absorbed in vehicles scrapped in 1923. By 1930 that figure had increased to 100%.[48] In 1923 domestic auto sales increased from the previous year by nearly 1.4 million units. In 1930 domestic auto sales *decreased* from the previous by more than 1.6 million units. Clearly, one major difference between 1923 and 1930 was that in 1923 a much greater percentage of new car purchases were made by first time buyers.

This section has delineated the factors which condition the household attitude toward debt and has assessed the relative importance of each factor. One determinant of the attitude toward debt was defined as "the assessment by the household of its ability to make good on newly created cash flow commitments which result from installment borrowing." An important theme of this chapter is that the household borrowing decision is subject to uncertainty in the Knight-Keynes-Shackle meaning of the term. The ability to make good on debt obligations which come due at future dates cannot be predicted on the basis of probabilistic calculations. The following sections will describe the way in which the element of uncertainty enters in to the household borrowing decision and evaluate the significance of uncertainty in the household borrowing decision for the short run stability or instability of consumer durable spending.

3.3 RISK, UNCERTAINTY, AND THE HOUSEHOLD BORROWING DECISION

An installment debt contract is an instrument which legally obligates the household to make a series of cash disbursements (which are generally fixed in money terms) at set of specified future dates.[49] Because installment debt contracts are legally enforceable, failure to meet the terms of the contract on the part of the household entails repercussions which can be monetary or nonmonetary. The consequences of defaulting on an installment debt contract can include the forfeiture of assets taken as collateral on the loan as well as the payment of collection costs, attorneys fees and court costs. The courts may order the seizure of household property or the garnishment of future income to satisfy creditors. Moreover, the failure to meet debt obligations usually results in damage to individual credit ratings which adversely affects the ability to obtain finance in the future.

Based on the cost of defaulting, both monetary and otherwise, it seems clear that in almost every case individuals enter into debt obligations with the prior intention of meeting their commitments. Some might argue that the option of Chapter 7 bankruptcy increases the likelihood of a moral hazard problem with regard to consumer borrowing. That is, it might be the case that some borrowers, knowing that they can later take refuge under the bankruptcy laws, enter into installment debt contracts with no intention of meeting their obligations. Such cases can probably be dismissed as being extremely rare in light of the financial and psychological trauma which usually accompanies bankruptcy proceedings. Given that households fully intend to make good on contractual cash flow obligation pursuant to installment debt contracts at the point in time at which they enter into them, does it follow that the household is absolutely certain of its *ability* to meet such obligations? That is, can a particular borrower ever be completely certain of his/her ability to make, say, a $250 car payment due 48 months hence? If the household borrowing decision were completely free of uncertainty, the following facts must be true: (1) The future income stream of the household (extending into the future for a period at least as long as the maturity of existing or newly created obligations) must be capable of exact prediction; (2) the stream of future household expenditures must be capable of exact prediction; and (3) there must be no uncertainty as to the future spot price, or liquidity, of financial or tangible assets held by the household.

The statement that conditions (1) through (3) as given above in reality never hold would not provoke an argument. However, a distinctive feature of the new general equilibrium approach to business cycle theory as well as modern welfare economics is the underlying principle that the problem of decision making under uncertainty can be approached in the general context of probability theory. That is to say, the element of uncertainty is taken to be reducible to actuarial risk. The logical implication of this view is that, although a particular household borrower does not know within 100% certainty if in fact he/she will be capable of discharging debt obligations as they come due, the household can, on the basis of actuarial calculations, attach a specific numerical value to its probability of default. The concept of "borrowers risk" then means that borrower *Z* has *X* probability of defaulting and 1-*X* probability of not defaulting. There are many unforeseen events which are capable of impinging upon the ability of consumer debtors to make good on installment obligations, e.g., unanticipated reductions in income due to the loss of employment, accident, or sickness. Moreover, there could be unforeseen expenditures owing to damages to one's property, medical bills, or unanticipated tax liabilities. The spot price of financial or tangible assets the household had planned to liquidate in order to satisfy creditors might have fallen to levels which were not expected. The question is: Can the probability of any single event, or any combination of events, which, if they were to happen, would result in default on the part of the installment borrowers, be ascertained through the application of actuarial science. For those committed to the New Classical or modern welfare economics, the answer to the question is unambiguously yes.[50] Furthermore, the existence of an Arrow-Debreu complete set of future markets for contingent claims allows the household the option of contracting out of borrower's risk in much the same manner as the importer or exporter can shift the burden of exchange rate risk through contracting in the forward exchange market.

In fact, actuarial calculations are a poor guide to action in the case of the household decision to borrow. Shackle has outlined the conditions under which actuarial considerations serve as an appropriate guide to action:

> The conditions can be epitomized by two statements:
>
> (1) The frequency ratios, unless derived a priori, must have been obtained from a set of performances sufficiently uniform and sufficiently numerous. This condition may be satisfied in varying degrees and will accordingly give answers of varying precision. We must notice that the experience or the set of performances from which the frequency-ratios are obtained need not have been suffered or made by the person who proposes to use the knowledge.
>
> (2) The experiment, to the valuation of whose outcome the frequency-ratios are to be applied, must be what I shall call a divisible (in ital.) experiment.[51]

Shackle classifies an experiment as divisible

> when an experiment is such that its results will be obtained by adding together the results of a series of separate performances, and when these performances are going to be sufficiently uniform in their circumstances, and sufficiently numerous, for frequency-ratios derived from a past series of similar performances to be applied.[52]

Though an individual might, in principle at least, borrow frequently enough in the course of a lifetime such that the number of observations is sufficient to form a meaningful probability distribution with regard to his/her likelihood of default on a specific loan, the household decision to borrow is nonetheless *not* a divisible experiment. The household decision to borrow is a nondivisible experiment because the specific circumstances in place at the point in time of the borrowing decision are unique to that point in time and differ from those circumstances which were applicable to any past borrowing decision. Any factor relevant to calculating the probability of default on a given installment instrument, e.g., the age, health, stage of career development or income of the prospective borrower, as well as current economic conditions, are never the same at different points in calendar time. Hence an individual cannot logically make the statement: "Whereas in the past I have borrowed on fifty occasions and have been in default on only one occasion, I estimate the probability of my defaulting on newly created debt obligations is two percent." Inasmuch as each of the fifty "experiments" were performed under different circumstances, they lack the uniformity required to render such a probability distribution meaningful. The term "borrower's risk" turns out to be something of a misnomer in that it implies that the likelihood that the borrower will be unable to meet installment debt obligations is capable of actuarial calculation.[53] What passes for uncertainty is in truth knowledge.

3.4 UNCERTAINTY AND DEBT DEFLATION

Given that the household borrowing decision is subject to uncertainty, what are the implications with respect to the volume of durable spending or the level of business activity in general? Minsky (1975) has refined Keynesian investment theory by treating the firm analytically as a "liability structure," i.e., an institution which takes positions in physical capital assets by entering into legally enforceable debt instruments which contractually obligate the firm to a stream of payments which are typically fixed in money terms. Investment spending therefore often requires that the firm add liabilities to its existing debt structure. Thus, the investment decision is conditioned by the following factors: (1) The stream of revenues or quasi-rents which the firm derives from positions already taken in tangible assets; (2) expectations concerning revenues deriving from newly proposed investment projects; and, most importantly, (3) the revenues from ongoing productive activity of the firm as well as newly contemplated ventures in relation to existing liability structure of the firm. That is to say that decision makers within the firm must be convinced that current and anticipated cash flows are sufficient to "justify" the debt exposure of the firm before they are willing to commit the firm to positions in newly produced durable assets.

Conceptually, suppose that the balance sheets of all firms which make up the private sector were consolidated. A gradual deterioration of the consolidated balance sheet could have disastrous consequences in terms of a contraction of investment spending. A gradual deterioration of the balance sheet means that current and anticipated cash flows bear a progressively less desirable relationship to the firm's contractual debt obligations. If firms on average regard the existing debt structure as unwarranted in light of the current or projected earnings stream, a process described by Minsky as "debt deflation" might ensue.[54] Debt deflation occurs when firms adjust balance sheets to reflect a change in current or expected future earnings. A contemporaneous development would be a decline in spending for newly produced investment goods as decision makers within the firm are reluctant to layer balance sheets with additional cash flow obligations.

Could a similar principle be applied to the household sector, i.e., can the household be treated analytically as a liability structure which is subject to the phenomena of debt deflation? Yes, but there are some important qualifications. First, with the exception of mortgage borrowing, debts created in order to take positions in physical assets tend to be much longer term where the firm is concerned. A second point of contrast pertains to the reversibility of commitments in durable goods. Producer durables in general are heterogeneous and nondivisible and as such secondary markets, when they exist, tend to be thin and poorly organized. Hence in the case of producers durables, there will ordinarily be a high degree of uncertainty as to their future spot price and liquidity. The same thing can be said about consumer durables but there are important exceptions. Probably the most well developed secondary markets for durable goods are found in the used-car industry.[55] While these markets are not comparable in structure with secondary markets for other financial assets, households will in most cases have the option of selling their car if circumstances make it necessary. Of course it will be true in many instances that the proceeds from the sale of a used car will not be sufficient to retire remaining installment debt liabilities which were collateralized by the car sold. Nonetheless, consumer durable goods, and particularly automobiles, as a rule possess a greater degree of liquidity than do producer durables.[56] Still, the element of irreversibility is important when considering the purchase of a durable good. If the purchase of a durable good were perfectly reversible, or nearly so, then it follows that there would be a high degree of substitutability between money, financial assets, and durable goods as a store of value. Section 2.3 of Chapter 2 outlined the reasons why this is not the case.

When households are treated as liability structures, the outstanding debt liabilities are enormous. For example, installment liabilities alone amounted to 20% of disposable income in 1986. Mortgage debt outstanding by U.S. households was greater than 2 trillion, which was equal to 76% of personal disposable income in 1985.[57] And these figures do not include other debts such as personal loans which are very substantial in amount. The debt exposure of the household sector gives rise to the possibility of debt deflation whenever households on average view existing debt obligations as unwarranted given current or expected income flows which, in the case of the household, primarily take the form of wages and salaries. Uncertainty as to future income flows as well as the future spot price and liquidity of household assets results in a general reluctance to layer balance sheets with additional debt obligations and produces a slump in durable goods spending.

As an empirical matter, how does one detect the debt deflation phenomena from published time series data? A decline in the absolute level of debt outstanding or even a decline in the rate of growth of household liabilities, would seem to constitute evidence of debt deflation. However, this would be a false inference if a decline in outstanding debt or the volume of new credit extensions were in reality a reflection of a change in the willingness of financial institutions to accommodate the household demand for finance. Perhaps the best indicator would be the ratio of repayments to outstanding debt. Assuming that the average maturity of debts is not decreasing, an increase in this ratio would seem to indicate that households are attempting to reduce their overall indebtedness. Another indicator would be changes in the volume of repayments on revolving credit charges. Repayment schedules on revolving debt tend to be more flexible than those attached to other installment debt. Hence, debt deflation might manifest in a decline in the revolving use of credit card accounts.

3.5 THE EFFECT OF TAX LAWS

Another factor mentioned as a possible influence on the household attitude toward debt was tax provisions applying to the deductibility of interest charges or sales taxes incurred on durable goods purchases.

Prior to 1987, interest payments on installment debt contracts were fully deductible on individual tax returns for those who itemized. The Tax Reform Act of 1986 called for the gradual phase-out of nonmortgage interest deductions. In tax year 1987 50% of interest payments were deductible. That figure fell to 40% in 1988, 20% in 1989, and 10% in 1990. In tax year 1991 the deductibility of nonmortgage interest payments was completely phased-out.

Will the new tax law result in a significant decrease in installment borrowing and spending? Probably not. In 1981, only 3.3% of individual tax returns claimed itemized deductions for nonmortgage interest.[58]

3.6 SUMMARY

The argument has been made in the present chapter that monetary phenomena do influence the volume of spending for consumer durable goods. The importance of monetary factors derives essentially from the fact that in modern monetary economies spending units are liquidity-constrained and as such two key determinants of the volume of consumer expenditure are the willingness of households to incur debt obligations and the price and general availability of household finance. Section 3.1 set forth an interpretation of the household budget constraint which is fully consistent with a realistic conception of the nature of banking institutions and bank activities. The "household liquidity constraint" was presented as an alternative to the budget constraint of Walrasian General Equilibrium Theory. The remaining sections were devoted to a discussion of the factors which condition the attitude of the household sector toward debt obligations with particular emphasis placed on the element of uncertainty, as distinct from actuarial risk, and potential instability of consumer spending.

In section 3.1 autonomous consumption expenditure, or C_2, was taken to be a function of four arguments, one of which was defined as "the access of the household sector to finance." Chapter 4 is devoted to a discussion of supply-side conditions in consumer installment credit markets, or more specifically, the factors which condition the ability and/or willingness of commercial banks and other installment lenders to accommodate the demand of the household sector for finance. Chapter 4 will set the stage for a thorough examination of the effects of Federal Reserve policy on conditions in installment credit markets which is the subject of Chapter 6.

NOTES

1. Robinson (1979), p. 56.

2. Keynes (1936), *p. 162.*

3. The Rational Expectations (R.E.) approach to business cycle theory has sometimes been interpreted as a "superneutrality" of money position. However, abstracting from all other possible stochastic shocks to economy, deviations from the "natural rate" of output and employment can only occur if unanticipated money introduces "noise" into price signals. Moreover, proponents of R.E. do not rule out the possibility that agents make forecasting errors. Rather, it is presumed that agents do not make systematic errors. In the parlance of the econometrician, the residuals taken from the money forecasting equation are uncorrelated. For a discussion, see Lucas (1983).

4. Keynes, *op. cit.*, pp. 298-294.

5. Hicks has argued that there is no such thing as money in barter economies. Rather, in attempting to analyze pure exchange economies, the economist has imposed a numeraire. For example, Hicks states: "The numeraire is not money; it is not even partial money; it is not even assumed by the traders themselves as a unit of account. It is not more than a unit of account which the observing economist is using for his own purpose of explaining to himself what the traders are doing." See Hicks (1974), p. 3.

6. Money is neutral when a change in the nominal quantity of money has no effect on the rate of utilization of productive capacity but only on the prices of goods and services.

7. The neutrality or nonneutrality of money on real output (income) and employment in Walrasian auction markets is a nonsensical issue since these magnitudes are determined prior to the start of trading. The process of tatonnement merely sorts out the scheme of relative prices which reveal the "true" underlying excess demand functions of the traders. Nevertheless, several writers have approached the problem of money neutrality in a general equilibrium framework. Patinkin (1965) is the classic example.

8. The above account of nonmonetary, or barter, economies is not intended to be descriptive of any real-world economies, past or present. Also, the discussion should not be interpreted to suggest that monetary economies somehow represent a "natural" or "inevitable" progression from nonmonetary economies. Rather, the intent of the discussion is to bring to light the essential institutional features of monetary economies which have implications for the role of money in the consumption function.

9. Clower (1967), p. 86.

10. See Davidson (1978), p. 149.
11. *Ibid.*, pp. 151-152.
12. Von Mises (1935), p. 177.
13. Keynes (1930), Book 1, Chapter 2, p. 24.
14. See Clower (1965), p. 119.
15. Friedman and Schwartz, for example, state: "The interest rate is not the price of money; it is the price of credit." See Friedman and Schwartz (1982), Chapter 3. For a recent statement of this view, see Greenfield and Yeager (1986).
16. For example, Basil Moore has presented evidence that about one-half of the credit supplied by commercial banks is in the form of overdraft privileges extended to households, firms, or government units, and only about one-half of these are utilized at any point in time. See Moore (1984).
17. Keynes, *op. cit.*, Book 1, Chapter 3, p. 41.
18. See Keynes (1936), Chapter 8.
19. Consequently, postwar research on the consumption function has been directed at a different set of problems. For instance, a large body of postwar research is concerned with explaining cross sectional differences in household spending behavior. In addition, a problem commanding considerable attention is the apparent paradox involving the short run and secular behavior of the average propensity to consume brought to light by the work of Kuznets (1948).
20. Minsky (1975), p. 23.
21. The Gini coefficient is a versatile indicator which can be used to measure the size distribution of firms in an industry, the equality of income distribution, or as in the above case, the equality of wealth distribution. The Gini coefficient can assume values equal to or greater than zero and less than one. A value of zero corresponds to perfect equality of income, wealth distribution, etc.
22. See Chapter 2, section 2.3 for evidence on this point.
23. One way to avoid the "distress" sale of household property is by borrowing against the value of illiquid assets. In fact, it might be argued that home equity *is* a liquid asset since it is an asset which can often be used to collateralize personal loans. Interest rates on home equity loans can in a sense be viewed as the rate at which home equity can be discounted. Home equity lending is one of the fastest growing segments of the consumer finance industry. See Bennett (1985), p. 1.
24. Source: *1983 Survey of Consumer Finances*. Several writers argue that this figure overstates the actual volume of household borrowing in so far as it includes credit card charges. This is because

some credit card holders are strictly "convenience" users, i.e., these holders take advantage of grace periods to avoid interest or finance charges. Implicit in this reasoning is the view that one cannot be properly regarded as a borrower if one does not pay interest. Hence convenience users are not really borrowers and the proportion of credit card charges which constitute borrowing on the part of credit card holders depends on the percent of outstanding credit card debt which is repaid within the grace period, which typically runs 30 days or more. The logic of this argument is faulty in the following way: the purchase of a consumer good on a credit card establishes a legal obligation to pay a particular sum at a future date. It is immaterial whether the sum to be paid by the credit card user includes an interest or finance charge. Moreover, to the extent that the average balance of "convenience" users increases with time, then it must be the case that additional consumption expenditure is being made possible through consumer credit expansion.

25. Marshall (1930), Book IV, p. 234.

26. Keynes, *op. cit.*, pp. 28-29.

27. Keynes never explicitly stated that household borrowing was unimportant with respect to the level of aggregate demand; however, in Book III of the *General Theory*, "The Propensity to Consume," there is no mention of household borrowing, access to credit, or the attitude toward debt as factors influencing the propensity to consume out of a given level of income.

28. See, for example, Luckett (1982), p. 285, and Bennett, op. cit.

29. This statement cannot be made uncategorically. For example, some households may obtain personal loans in order to meet obligations on loans previously outstanding. Except in the case where loans are used to finance interest payments (Ponzi finance), loans used to pay off other loans are, in effect, "rolling over" and hence do not result in an increase in total loans outstanding. Also, some individuals may incur debt for speculative purposes such as in the case of loans extended by brokers.

30. Under the Truth in Lending Act of 1981, consumer installment lenders are required to calculate and disclose interest charges based on the annual percentage rate (APR) formula.

31. The problem of price formation in consumer credit and durable goods markets is discussed in Chapter 4.

32. A related consideration would be the costs of bankruptcy, pecuniary and otherwise. The problem of household borrowing and bankruptcy is taken up in section 3.4.

33. For example, George W. Norris, Governor of the Federal Reserve Board of Philadelphia, commenting on installment credit: "It is born of the seller's passion for volume and the buyer's passion for indulgence." See Norris (1926), p. 212.

34. See Keynes, *op. cit.*, p. 100.

35. Davidson, *op. cit.*, p. 411.

36. There are exceptions, e.g., the use of the family car to deliver newspapers.

37. Source: *Ward's Automotive Yearbook* and the *Federal Reserve Bulletin*.

38. Source: Oak Ridge National Laboratory, *Scrappage and Survival Rates of Passenger Cars and Trucks*.

39. For example, the period 1950-1970 was one of generally expanding auto sales. Suppose that auto sales increase every year for five years. Under these conditions the average age of a passenger car in use will decline each year even if scrappage rates are constant because a greater percentage of total cars in use will be less than one year old.

40. For a discussion, see Adams and Brock (1986), pp. 141-144.

41. See, for example, Kowalewski (1986), and Forrestall (1987).

42. The size of durables stock can in principle be measured in two ways: (1) By summing the number of units of cars, vacuum cleaners, etc., and multiplying the total by current market value; and (2) valuing the stock of durables at its depreciated value. Almost without exception, researchers have used the latter method of calculation. See, for example, Williams (1972), Mishkin (1976), and Kendrick (1976).

43. Williams, *op. cit.*, p. 281.

44. See Veblen (1945), and Duesenberry, *op. cit.*

45. A recent example would be the development and marketing of fuel efficient vehicles and home appliances in the mid to late 1970s. There was a strong surge in replacement demand for automobiles in the recovery from the 1974-1975 recession as consumers switched from luxury and intermediate size cars to fuel efficient compacts and subcompacts.

46. For a discussion of the industry life-cycle hypothesis, see Porter (1980), pp. 156-158.

47. Schumpeter views the process of creative destruction as the "essential fact about capitalism." See Schumpeter (1952), p. 83. Schumpeter describes this process as "the opening of new markets, foreign or domestic, and the organizational development from the craft shop and factory to such concerns as U.S. Steel illustrate the same

process of industrial mutation--if I may use a biological term--that incessantly revolutionizes the economic structure from with (in ital.), incessantly destroying the old one, incessantly creating a new one." *Ibid*, p. 83. With respect to groundswell effects: "These revolutions periodically reshape the existing structure of industry by introducing new methods of production--the mechanized factory, the electrified factory, chemical synthesis and the like; new commodities, such as railroad service, motor cars, electric appliances; new forms of organization--the merger movement; new sources of supply--La Plata wool, American copper, Katanga copper; new trade routes and markets to sell in and so on. This process of industrial change provides the groundswell that gives the general tone of business; while these things are being initiated we have brisk expenditure and predominating 'prosperity'--interrupted, no doubt, by the negative phases of the shorter cycles which are superimposed on that groundswell--while those things are being completed and their results pour forth we have the elimination of antiquated elements of the industrial structure and predominating 'depression.'" *Ibid.*, p. 68.

48. Source: *Auto Facts and Figures*, 22nd ed., 1939. The ratio of replacement vehicles to total domestic demand averaged 32.3% in the period 1921-1925, 61.3% between 1926-1929, and 85% in the years 1930-1939.

49. The term "cash disbursements" should not be taken to mean that debtors fulfill obligations through direct payment of legal tender to creditors. Rather, it is intended to apply to the process of check clearing whereby the borrower's bank account is debited and the lender's credited.

50. Overlapping generation models posit the existence of an optimizing agent with an infinite lifespan, given an "operable" bequest motive. Such models typically incorporate the assumption of perfect foresight (or the presumable weaker assumption, i.e., rational expectations) to prove the neutrality of debt-financed government expenditure on the intertemporal consumption plan of a "representative" agent. See, for instance, Barro, op. cit., and McCallum (1984). Feldstein has recently shown that the "Ricardian Equivalence" theorem does not hold in the case where agents have no knowledge about income flows accruing to future generations. See Feldstein (1988).

51. Shackle (1955), p. 4.

52. *Ibid.*, p. 5.

53. The argument is made in Chapter 4 that actuarial considerations *do* serve as an appropriate guide to action for banks, finance companies, etc. Lenders can pool the results of many individual

experiments and establish a reasonable accurate probability of default for a borrower with a given profile.

54. See Minsky (1985).

55. Other examples of secondary markets for consumer goods would be flea markets and garage sales.

56. Automobiles are of course an important producer good in many industries, e.g., the rental car industry. Thus automobiles as a producer good illustrate one exception to the general principle stated above.

57. Source: *Federal Reserve Bulletin*, Domestic Financial Statistics, Table A376.

58. Source: *Federal Reserve Bulletin*, June 1985, p. 17.

Chapter 4

The Installment Lenders

In Chapter 3, section 3.1, total consumption expenditure was decomposed into two categories, namely: (1) Consumer spending which depends on current income (C_1), and (2) consumer spending which depends on factors other than income (C_2). Consumer spending put into the category of C_2 was in turn posited to be a function of four variables, two of which were defined as the price of consumer credit and the access of the household sector to finance. As was stated earlier, in an economy in which a substantial proportion of consumer durable goods purchases are debt-financed, the volume of durable spending is crucially dependent on a regularized flow of credit extensions to the household sector. Thus the diverse group of business concerns which make up the installment credit industry take an integral role in sustaining the level of effective demand.

Chapter 4 is divided into five sections. Section 4.1 describes the structure of the installment credit industry. The distribution of consumer receivables and lending activities among commercial banks, finance companies, credit unions, retailers, and savings and loan institutions is analyzed. Section 4.2 explores the various factors which determine the ability and/or willingness of installment lenders to hold consumer installment receivables in their portfolios of earning assets. Section 4.3 is concerned with the problem of price formation in the installment credit industry. The problem is approached through the application of partial equilibrium analysis to the price and quantity decisions of a "representative" installment lender. Finally, the effects of legal usury ceilings on both the price and quantity supplied of installment credit is discussed.

4.1 STRUCTURE OF THE INSTALLMENT CREDIT INDUSTRY

Figure 4-1 shows the share of total consumer installment credit outstanding held by commercial banks, finance companies, credit unions, and retailers in selected years. Installment credit is defined as short or intermediate term credit that is scheduled to be repaid (or has the option of repayment) in two or more installments.[1]

Commercial banks are a major force in determining both the volume of consumer credit and the terms on which such credit is granted. Though the average commercial bank holds only about 10% of its portfolio of earning assets in the form of loans collateralized by consumer goods, commercial banks collectively held 41% of outstanding installment rate in 1970 and 47% in 1980. Moreover, these figures understate the importance of commercial banks in consumer credit markets since other major supplies of consumer credit, mainly finance companies and retailers, rely heavily on bank loans to finance positions in installment receivables. For example, in 1986 loans of commercial banks to nonbank financial institutions amounted to 35.6 billion dollars.[2] Banks are also engaged in the purchase of installment paper in the secondary market.[3]

Figure 4-2 gives the market shares of the various installment lenders in the auto loan market in selected years. Note that the combined share of finance companies in the auto loan market is greater than their share in the installment market at large. One explanation for this is that relative importance of the "captive" finance companies such as General Motors Acceptance Corporation or Ford Motors Acceptance Corporation in the market for automobile credit. Apart from the profitability of installment lending, auto manufacturers may have additional motives with respect to their diversification into the consumer credit business. Specifically, officers of the major auto concerns may want assurances that the flow of credit extensions to the household sector is both stable and sufficient to move inventories of finished automobiles at the desired rate. For this reason the diversification of durable goods manufacturers into the consumer finance industry might be viewed as a special case of vertical integration.

The structure of the installment credit industry is difficult to analyze. In 1983 in the U.S. there were over 14,500 commercial banks with consumer installment paper in their portfolios and more than 6,000 consumer finance companies. On the basis of these figures one might

Figure 4-1

Share of Installment Receivables Held by Consumer Lending Institutions, 1990

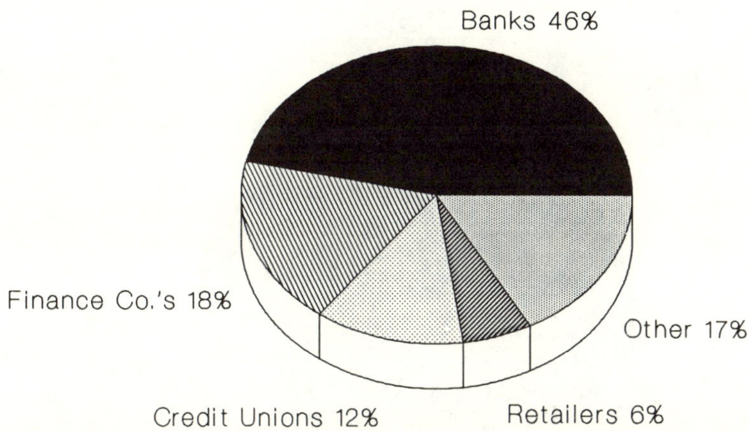

Other includes S&L's, gas co.'s, and mutual savings banks

Source: *Federal Reserve Bulletin*, Domestic Financial Statistics, Table 1.55.

Figure 4-2

Share of Auto Installment Receivables Held by Lending Institutions, 1984

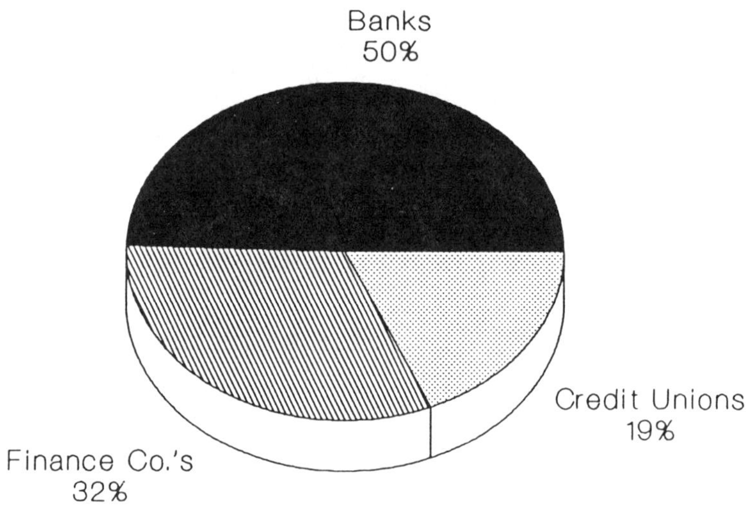

Source: *Federal Reserve Bulletin*, Domestic Financial Statistics, Table 1.56.

conclude that consumer credit markets are atomistic in structure and that consumer lenders are "price-takers." However, the size distribution of both banks and finance companies is very skewed. For example, the smallest 10,000 banks hold less than 16% of the total deposits of the commercial banking system. The largest 356 banks, or 2.5% of the banks in the U.S., hold 55% of all the deposits of the banking system. Of course, the predominant concern here is the distribution of commercial bank assets, as opposed to liabilities, among commercial banks and other installment lenders. In 1982, the largest 56 banks, or 0.5% of all banks, controlled 41.8% of total U.S. commercial bank assets. The largest 281 banks collectively hold 67.1% of total assets. Table 4-1 shows the asset size distribution of U.S. commercial banks.

Table 4-1

Asset Size Distribution of U.S. Commercial Banking Organizations (December 31, 1982)

Size Class (in millions of $)	Number of Organizations	Percent of Banks	Percentage of Total U.S. Commercial Bank Assets
0-5	428	3.4	0.1
5-10	1,405	11.5	0.5
10-25	3,837	31.3	3.3
25-100	4,968	40.5	12.0
100-250	923	7.5	6.9
250-500	246	2.0	4.3
500-1000	170	1.4	5.9
1000-5000	225	1.8	25.3
5000+	56	0.5	41.8

Source: Board of Governors, Federal Reserve System.

Though there are no data concerning the distribution of installment debt among commercial banks, one would be inclined to think that the majority of installment debt outstanding is held by the largest 250 banks. Table 4-2 shows consumer loans outstanding held by two large U.S. commercial banks (Citicorp and Chemical Banking Corporation) and one smaller regional bank (Firstar, formerly First Wisconsin). Note that consumer loans outstanding accounted for 31.0% of total loans outstanding at Citicorp on December 31, 1988. This is an extraordinarily high figure for a commercial bank and does not reflect the typical organization of loan portfolios at moneycenter banks. The data for Chemical Banking Corporation represents a closer approximation of lending practices at most banks. Nevertheless, the data are generally consistent with the view that the installment lending industry is far more concentrated than one would be given to believe on the basis of the absolute number of installment lenders alone.

Table 4-2

Consumer Loans Outstanding Held by Selected U.S. Commercial Banks

Institution	Consumer Loans Outstanding on December 31, 1988 (in millions)	Total Loans Outstanding on December 31, 1988 (in millions)	Consumer Loans as a Percent of Total Loans Outstanding
Citicorp	$44,944	$144,992	31.0
Chemical Banking Corporation	4,549	41,590	10.9
Firstar	1,750	4,903	35.7

Source: 1988 *Annual Reports* of Citicorp, Chemical Banking Corporation, and Firstar.

Similarly, total assets held by consumer finance companies tend to be highly concentrated in the portfolios of the largest firms. According to R. A. Gilbert, the 50 largest finance companies, measured in terms of assets held, controlled more than 70% of assets held by all U.S. based finance companies.[4] These figures understate the actual degree of market concentration in the installment credit industry since the geographic extent of the market is not national in scope.[5] In fact, most economists view the geographic market for broadly defined "banking services" as local or regional in scope.[6]

Market concentration, as measured by the percent of total deposits held by an absolute number of the largest banks, is much greater if the geographic extent of the market is defined as being local rather than national. For example, the three largest commercial banks in New York City held 48% of total deposits in that market in 1981. In Atlanta, the top three banks held 65.6% of total deposits.[7] Burke estimated that the average four firm concentration ratio for 60 standard metropolitan statistical areas, i.e., the share of total deposits held by the four largest banks in an SMSA, was 80.7% in 1982.[8]

It is not necessarily the case that the geographic extent of the market for installment credit is coextensive with the market for other banking services. For instance, while there are many legal restrictions on the geographic extent of the market for consumer demand deposits, there are no legal restrictions applicable to the geographic extent of the market for installment lending. So whereas Chase Manhattan cannot hold demand deposits in Tennessee, it may issue credit cards or make car loans to Tennessee residents. Heggestad and Shepard commented on this issue as follows:

> Banks offer many products to different types of consumers. Depending on the size and the type of transaction, the geographic market for the bank product will differ considerably. The market for consumer-demand deposits, where convenience is the most important factor, may be as small as a neighborhood or a section of a city. Conversely, the market for large commercial loans will cover the entire nation. Bank borrowers and lenders will find it in their interest to arrange transactions irrespective of location. The bulk of commercial banking operations, however, including financial services sold to most households and small businesses, is limited to a fairly small geographic area, such as a city or a rural county.[9]

Again, the structure of the installment credit industry is very difficult to pin down in the manner preferred by Industrial Organization economists. According to the taxonomy set forth by Shepard, the structure of the installment credit industry probably falls somewhere between "tight oligopoly" and "effective competition."[10] For Shepard, a market structure is characterized by tight oligopoly if the four-firm concentration ratio exceeds 60%, with stable market shares, and a tendency toward cooperation or collusion on the part of sellers. A market is "effectively competitive" if the four-firm concentration below is 40% with unstable market shares and flexible pricing. In reality the installment credit industry probably defies this type of categorization. The data do support the conclusion that the market for installment credit is not perfectly competitive in structure and that installment lenders do possess some degree of power over price. However, the degree of market power possessed by the large installment lenders as measured by, for example, the Lerner Index, is very difficult to ascertain.[11]

4.2 FACTORS DETERMINING THE WILLINGNESS OF LENDERS TO HOLD CONSUMER RECEIVABLES

The ability of commercial banks and other financial institutions to accommodate the finance requirements of economic agents in both the private and public sector depends on a complex set of social and institutional factors as well as the technology of the payments process. Included among these are the confidence of the public in the integrity of the banking system, the existence of mechanisms to facilitate the clearing of bank debts, the existence of fluid interbank reserve markets, and the existence of facilities for the discounting of bank assets. A factor of decisive importance in a system based on the fractional reserve principle is obviously the willingness of the Central Bank to accommodate the need for reserves by commercial banks.[12] This is accomplished primarily by the purchase of government securities on the open market or the discounting of bank assets by the Federal Reserve Bank. The relationship between Federal Reserve policy, conditions in installment credit markets, and the volume of consumer spending is the subject of Chapter 6.

This section is concerned with the factors which determine the willingness of lending institutions to hold consumer installment receivables. As a general principle, assets are held because they yield income or because they possess liquidity. While it is true that short-term Treasury bills yield interest, they are held in bank portfolios primarily because they are a source of liquidity. Owing to the organization of the secondary market for short-term government debt, there is a high degree of certainty as to the liquidity of Treasury issues. For this reason bank portfolio managers probably view their holdings of government securities as a secondary source of bank reserves. Consumer installment paper is held because it yields income. Installment receivables are part of a bank's portfolio of earning assets. Hence the primary determinant of the willingness of banks to make credit extensions to households is the profitability of holding installment receivables as compared to the profitability of other lines of business such as commercial and industrial lending.

The profitability of holding installment paper is determined by the spread between the lenders' cost of funds and the interest rate charged on consumer loans. Additional costs to consider would be the administrative cost of processing loan applications as well as allowances made for collection costs, attorneys fees, and charge-offs due to default. For banks, lender's cost consist mainly of interest payments made on interest-earning checkable deposits as well as savings and time deposits. Other costs would include the discount rate applied on advances from Federal Reserve banks as well as the rate paid on funds raised in the federal funds market. Lenders' cost for credit unions and thrifts would consist of mostly the same costs born by commercial banks. Finance companies take positions in installment paper through bank loans, the issue of commercial paper, and in the case of the largest companies, the issue of long term bonds.

Are lender's costs sensitive to movements in the complex of short-term interest rates? It depends on the maturity structure of liabilities carried by installment lenders. For instance, if the liabilities of a finance company consist mainly of long-term bank loans or bonds then a substantial proportion of lender's cost will be fixed in money terms. It is a different story for banks. A large quantity of bank deposits are claims held by firms or government units. The past twenty years have witnessed an increase in the sophistication of cash-management techniques as well as the development of deep markets for highly liquid money substitutes. Hence banks run the risk of a portfolio shift of major depositors out of bank money in response to an increase in interest rates in the market for short-term debt. To reduce this risk, banks must offer rates which are competitive with those carried by the assortment of money substitutes. Given that the income stream deriving from installment receivables is essentially fixed in money terms, it follows that, for banks in particular, the profitability of consumer lending is sensitive to short term interest rates. This point becomes important when examining the effects of Federal Reserve policy on the willingness of banks to accommodate household credit demand.[13]

Apart from the profitability of holding installment receivables, consumer lending activities offer a means by which bank officers can diversify the bank's portfolio of earning assets. Because the typical installment loan is small in amount compared to average loan amounts on commercial and industrial loans, an installment loan to a particular household involves minimal exposure of the bank to a single borrower, a practice consistent with what are generally thought to be sound banking principles. A bank achieves much greater diversification if it makes ten $10,000 car loans to ten different households than if it makes one $100,000 loan to a single business customer.[14]

As was argued in Chapter 3 the probability of default for a single household borrower cannot be ascertained through the application of actuarial science. A health insurance company cannot estimate the probability a person with a given health profile will have of suffering a heart attack within two years. However, if there are 10,000 persons with basically the same health profile, the insurance company can estimate with reasonably good accuracy the number of persons in that group likely to have heart attacks within two years. This is the principle of insurance. It is the task of actuaries to pool the results of case histories for thousands of persons fitting various health profiles and then formulate probability distributions concerning the incidence of various health problems within each group.

Similarly, installment lenders cannot predict the likelihood that a particular borrower will default based on information such as the borrower's age, income, education level, length of employment, credit history, liquid assets held, or other factors. What installment lenders can know with reasonable accuracy is this: If credit extensions were made to 1,000 households with a given credit profile, how many would default? To say that default rates can be predicted with reasonable accuracy means that in most circumstances the number of household borrowers which *actually* default will not depart substantially from the number of household borrowers *expected* to default based on the credit history of borrowers with a similar credit profile. In formal statistical terms, there is a density function which describes the probability of various default rates actually occurring. Default rates are reasonably predictable because the density function exhibits low dispersion around its mean value, i.e., the variance of the distribution is comparatively low.

It should be noted that a given density function is based on a *given* value of aggregate income. For example, a decline in national income due to a contraction of business activity would render borrowers more risky on average. This conclusion follows from the fact that the level of disposable income is the vital determinant of the ability to repay debt obligations. Hence, a contraction in national income can be expected to result in a decrease in the average disposable income of borrowers with consequent adverse effect on their ability to pay. The importance of this phenomena is evidenced by the countercyclical behavior of default rates on consumer installment loans. Commercial banks and other installment lenders can expect an increase in bad debt losses in the event of a cyclical downturn in economic activity.

Aside from complications arising from changing macroeconomic conditions, actuarial calculations do serve as an appropriate guide to action in the case of installment lenders. That is, charge offs and other costs related to bad debt write-offs can be predicted reasonably well so long as the installment lender has a diverse portfolio of consumer installment paper. Moreover, installment lenders should be able to roughly predict cost savings which would be realized through a tightening of the minimum standards of credit worthiness.

The ability to predict bad debt losses on consumer lending operations is probably subject to a learning curve. That is, institutions which have been in the installment credit business for many years have vast experience in estimating charge offs per dollar lent for a given set of credit standards.

4.3 PRICING IN INSTALLMENT CREDIT MARKETS

The interest rate is the price of credit.[15] How does this price get determined in installment credit markets? The present section sets forth a simple theory of price formation in installment credit markets which is consistent with the Liquidity Preference theory of the interest rate as well as price-making behavior on the part of installment lenders.

In the perfect credit market of neoclassical interest theory, there is no rationing. Interest rate fluctuations are the mechanism by which the flow of available credit is allocated among competing borrowers. At the equilibrium interest rate, any one borrower may obtain all the credit that is desired at the prevailing interest rate. The shape of the supply curve of credit is given by the rate of time preference.[16] That is, the supply curve for finance is the schedule revealing the extent to which the community of savers is prepared to defer present consumption at each level of interest. Hence, abstracting from demand-side elements, the interest rate is determined by the habits of thrift prevailing in the economy at large. The presence of commercial banks, finance companies, and other lending institutions apparently does not render this principle invalid since these institutions are viewed as merely extending the chain of intermediation between savers and borrowers.[17] It is important to note that the equilibrium of neoclassical interest theory is a *flow*, as opposed to stock, equilibrium. The interest rate adjusts simultaneously to equate the current flow of saving and borrowing.

The Liquidity Preference theory of the rate of interest is based on the recognition that the predominant influence on the rate of interest is not the willingness of economic agents to defer present consumption, but rather the willingness of wealth-holding units to hold the outstanding stock of debt instruments. Keynes conceived of the equilibrium interest rate as a stock equilibrium. The neoclassical theory leads to the conclusion that yields on both previously issued debt instruments as well as newly issued liabilities are determined in the market for new placements. The Liquidity Preference theory proceeds from the insight that additions to the stock of debt obligations (new placements) in a given time period will be very small in comparison with the stock of debt obligations previously issued. Hence, yields on newly issued debt instruments must come into equality with yields on issues already held. Shackle described the implications of Keynes' insight:

> Within any brief interval we care to select, the quantity of old bonds that can be released for the purchase of bonds, by a change in the interest rate, is overwhelmingly greater than the quantity of net new borrowing and lending that might be induced by the same

> change. The market for old and new bonds combined is dominated by the vast stock of old bonds and by the great mass of money which at all times exists in the hands of those individuals or firms who for the moment fear a price-fall of securities. Against these pre-existing masses, always poised for release onto the market by any sufficient movement of the interest rate, little influence can be exerted by the quantities of new bond issues, or of savings newly accumulated, within a brief past interval, in the hands of those waiting to return them, via purchase (directly or indirectly) of new bond issues, to the business community. It is thus the interest rate, or the system of rates, can be too high to allow for full employment.[18]

Interest rates carried by bonds or other promises to pay must be sufficiently high to induce economic agents to hold wealth in the form of debt obligations as opposed to money. Interest is the "reward for parting with liquidity."[19]

The above analysis is concerned with the determination of interest rates on financial instruments which are dealt in highly developed secondary markets and thus possess a greater degree of liquidity than consumer installment receivables. As was stated earlier, the secondary market for installment paper is relatively well developed and the Federal Reserve will act as buyer of last resort under certain circumstances. However, the secondary market for installment paper is not comparable in structure with the market for, say, short-dated Treasury bills. It is for this reason that the price of installment credit *is not* determined by the willingness of economic agents to hold the outstanding stock of consumer debt. Owing to the absence of a continuous spot market with specialist traders acting as residual buyers and sellers of installment paper, there exists no set of forces which ensure that yields on newly created consumer debt obligations will come into equality with yields on installment paper already outstanding. Rather, installment lenders act as "price makers" in the market for consumer credit.

Given that the price of consumer credit is "administered" by lending institutions, what factors enter into the determination of administered prices? Commercial banks practice third degree price discrimination in their consumer lending operations. That is, consumers are segregated out as a special class of borrowers and are typically offered credit under a different set of terms than other classes of borrowers. However, it is not the ordinary practice of installment lenders to engage in first degree price discrimination. Lending institutions will typically offer credit on the same terms to all household borrowers deemed credit worthy. Lenders do not generally adjust interest rates to reflect differences in willingness to pay among households.[20] Nor is it the case that lenders will accommodate riskier borrowers at higher interest rates. Interest rate movements *are not* the mechanism by which credit is allocated among competing household borrowers. Consequently, there will always be a group of potential household borrowers which is unable to obtain installment credit on any terms.

Instead of thinking in terms of a market supply curve for consumer credit, it is appropriate to think of a "representative" bank or finance company which administers the price of installment credit. Section 4.1 described the structure of the installment credit industry. Evidence was presented in support of the proposition that the installment credit industry is imperfectly competitive in structure. Installment lenders face downward sloping demand schedules for credit and as such possess some degree of power over market price. The price of credit is determined by a mark-up over the estimated cost of holding installment receivables. Relevant costs would include the cost of processing loan applications, allowances made for collection costs, attorneys' fees, and bad debt write-offs, a charge made to cover allocated overhead costs, and other costs such as the payment of interest on bank liabilities, commercial paper, bank loans, or bonds. In the case of credit card operations, the maintenance of up-to-the-minute, worldwide authorization systems is a significant administrative cost.[21] The issue of what factors determine the mark-up over cost is a complicated one. If it is assumed that installment lenders are profit maximizers, then the administered interest rate is that rate which is expected to maximize the net earnings derived from holding installment receivables.

This analysis bears a resemblance to the mark-up pricing models attributable to writers such as Kalecki (1940) and Eichner (1976). Such models are based on the observation that in highly developed industrial economies the manufacturing core is dominated by large, vertically integrated firms which possess power over price. Under ordinary circumstances these firms will have reserve capacity which could be utilized if firms decide to increase the rate of output. Technical conditions are such that unit prime costs of production will remain roughly constant at different scales of output. Hence firms in most circumstances will not experience rising unit prime costs due to the principle of diminishing returns when the rate of capacity utilization is increased. Prices are determined by a mark-up over unit prime costs and firms stand ready to supply all the output the market will bear at the administered price. Firms are "price makers" and "quantity takers."

On one level, the mark-up pricing model is appropriate for analyzing price formation in consumer credit markets. Installment lenders do possess some market power and the activity of installment lending is not subject to the law of diminishing returns. However, installment lenders are in an important way quantity-makers as well as price-makers. Lenders are quantity-makers to the extent that they decide who shall get credit. Transactions in product markets involve the exchange of money for goods or services. Transactions in installment credit markets involve the exchange of promises to pay. The latter type of transaction s subject to a moral hazard problem. Refusal to deal is illegal under Section 3 of the Clayton Act of 1914. However, the law applies only to sellers of goods and services. Lenders may legally refuse to accommodate any borrower, so long as refusal to deal is not based on sex, color, race, political conviction, or religious persuasion. A supply curve of credit is relevant only to those households which meet some minimum standards of credit worthiness.

4.4 EFFECTS OF USURY CEILINGS

A complicated issue concerns the effect of usury ceilings on the hire-purchase terms and availability of consumer credit. In 1975 there were 48 states with usury ceilings on consumer loans. Ceilings ranged from a high of 41.7 "APR" in Mississippi to a low of 10% in Arkansas. It should be noted that usury laws apply mainly to open-ended or revolving credit. Interest rates on revolving or credit card debt tend to be 2 to 10 percentage points higher on average than rates on other installment loans. Though the terms interest rate and finance charge are used interchangeably here, spokespersons for major credit card issuers typically reject this interpretation. They cite the high administrative overhead costs carried by their credit card operations as the explanation for the spread on rates between open-ended credit and, say, the prime rate. The evidence does not appear to contradict this claim. For example, banks pay a fee to the two major credit card companies for the rights to issue credit cards under the Visa and Mastercard name as well as for access to the centralized billing service operated by these companies. Based on the Federal Reserve's 1973 functional cost analysis, administrative costs of commercial bank credit card operations were equal to 70% of the gross income deriving from those operations.[22]

In 1986 there was an attempt in the Senate to replace the myriad of state laws with the Federal usury legislation. Two bills were proposed. The National Credit Card Protection Act would impose a ceiling of 5 percentage points above the "index rate," which was to be average yield in the preceding calendar year on a six-month Treasury bill. Under the credit Care Holder Protection Act the rate on credit cards would be limited to 4 percentage points above the prime rate charged by banks in the previous six months. The use of an index rate is based on the assumption that changes in lender's cost are effectively mirrored in the movement of some short term rate selected as the index. Martha Seger of the Federal Reserve Board rejected this view:

> Turning to the specific provisions of the bill before Congress, it should be emphasized that credit cards are issued by a broad variety of retail merchants and financial institutions which differ both as to their sources of funding and their liability structure. Under these circumstances, a single index rate would be unlikely to mirror charges in the costs for such a diverse array of card issuers. In any case, short-term rates, such as the Treasury bill rate or the Federal Reserve discount rate, fluctuate a good deal more widely than costs of funds of most lenders. They do so because a lender's overall average cost of funds at any point is a blend of current interest rates and rates on previously issued liabilities, and because market rates on longer-term liabilities--which usually make up the cost of funds--typically vary less than short-term rates.[23]

The relationship between lenders' cost and the complex of short term interest rates is an important issue when examining the effect of open market operations on conditions in installment credit markets. If interest charges on installment contracts exhibit rigidities or do not adjust fluidly to changing conditions in the market for short term debt, then it follows that the profitability of holding installment receivables is sensitive to changes in lenders' cost. Moreover, if the FED can effectively target the rate prevailing in the interbank reserve market, i.e., the rate which perhaps most accurately reflects lenders' cost, then it may impact on the profitability of consumer lending operations. A full discussion of this issue is deferred to Chapter 6.

The rationing effect of a usury ceiling is most often illustrated with a supply-demand diagram and a price ceiling which falls below the intersection of competitive supply and demand functions. An upward sloping supply of credit schedule with respect to the interest rate is apparently consistent with the loanable funds (time preference) theory of the rate of interest. It is probably more appropriate to think of a "representative" bank or finance company which administratively determines the price of credit and stands ready to supply all the credit that is demanded by those borrowers who meet the minimum standards of credit worthiness. Again, factors influencing the pricing decision would include the cost of funds, the cost of processing loan applications, allowances made for charge offs, and the desired rate of return from the firm's holdings of consumer paper.

A legal usury ceiling will obviously affect the profitability of holding installment receivables if it falls below the rate which lenders have determined will maximize the earnings derived from their portfolios of installment paper. There are three possible reactions on the part of lenders to the imposition of a usury ceiling. The first would be to maintain the volume of credit extensions to households and accept a lower profit rate on consumer lending operations. The second would be to curtail, or even halt, credit extensions to households regardless of the credit worthiness of the set of potential borrowers. The second option is more likely to be taken by banks than finance companies since consumer lending is not a primary line of commerce. Hence, banks may shift to different types of loans in the event a usury ceiling is imposed. A third possible reaction on the part of lenders would be to attempt to restore profit rates on consumer lending operation through reductions in costs, specifically, collection costs and charge offs due to bad debt. This would be accomplished through a tightening of the minimum standards of credit worthiness. As was stated earlier, the risk of default on the part of a certain household borrower can be actualized reasonably well on the basis of factors such as income, credit history, length of employment, liquid assets held, and other outstanding debt obligations. Hence financial institutions can roughly predict cost savings in the form of reduced charge offs and collection costs that would be realized through a tightening of the minimum standards of credit worthiness. Credit rationing then takes the form of the crowding out of marginal borrowers under stricter credit standards.[24]

The literature concerning the effect of legal usury ceilings on credit availability is limited. The most frequently cited study is the Arkansas case study done by Lynch.[25] He concluded that the 10% usury ceiling had an adverse effect on the availability of credit to households, particularly low income households. There was a significant decline in credit cards issued by Arkansas banks. Lynch noted, however, that consumers often were able to substitute "point-of-sale" credit for credit offered by financial institutions. In the case of retail establishments which offer point of sale credit, usury ceilings can be effectively circumvented through an increase in retail prices. Lynch reported that retail prices for durable goods were "significantly higher" in Arkansas than in states with less restrictive usury ceilings. Conner and Fergus point out that retail establishments are not alone in their ability to adjust to usury ceilings through price increases:

> Although increases in merchandise prices can be implemented only by retailers, some issuers of bank credit cards might be able to effect an indirect form of repricing by raising the fee they charge merchants for processing credit card sales. The fee, called the merchant discount is an operating cost to the retailer. Any increase in these charges could be passed on in higher prices of merchandise, including prices paid by customers who always pay in cash.
>
> Other card-related fees could also be raised. Seventy percent of more of commercial banks in 1985 charged an annual fee for Mastercard and Visa accounts. These annual fees could be increased to help generate higher revenue, and additional institutions could implement such fees.[26]

Douglas Greer performed a series of regressions to determine the relationship between excess demand for credit, as measured by the rate at which loan applications are rejected by consumer finance companies, and interest rate ceilings.[27] Not surprisingly, for a sample covering 24 states Greer found an inverse relationship between permitted finance charges and loan rejections at consumer finance companies.

Are usury ceilings a good idea? The imposition of usury ceilings can have at least three potentially undesirable effects. First, it is possible that under certain circumstances usury ceilings could produce congestion in the market for installment credit with a reduction in the volume of consumer spending. Secondly, the evidence points to the fact that the adoption of such ceilings invariably results in a tightening of the minimum standards of credit worthiness. Such changes in credit policy adversely affects the ability of low income households, or households without an established credit history, to obtain finance. In the case where ceilings result in an increase in the prices of goods and services, those consumers which do not use credit must nonetheless feel the effects of the usury ceiling.

The Federal Reserve Board of Governors has been unwavering in its opposition to usury laws of any kind. Seger summarized the Board's view in a speech before the House Committee on Banking, Finance, and Urban Affairs on March 18, 1987:

> From experience with the imposition of credit controls in 1980 and the sharp, unexpected contraction in consumer spending that accompanied them, we know that regulatory measures can have unpredictable and unwanted consequences. Setting a federal ceiling on credit cards below those that currently prevail in many states would most likely reduce the amount of credit available, forcing consumers to rely instead upon less convenient and possibly more expensive substitutes or to lose access to credit at any rate. Moreover, such a curtailment would be apt to fall most heavily on less affluent borrowers with relatively limited access to other sources of credit.[28]

4.5 SUMMARY

This chapter has described and analyzed supply-side conditions in markets for consumer installment credit. First, though the installment credit industry is difficult to categorize from a structural standpoint, the evidence generally supports the thesis that the installment credit industry is imperfectly competitive in structure and that installment lenders are "price-makers." Second, the primary determinant of the willingness of installment lenders to make credit extensions to households is the profitability of holding installment receivables. The profitability of holding installment paper is determined by the spread between the lender's cost of funds and the interest rate charged on consumer loans. Third, bad debt write-offs on consumer installment loans are regarded as a normal business expense by lenders and can be predicted reasonably well. Fourth, the price of installment credit is "administered" by lenders on the basis of a mark-up over lender's cost. Finally, usury ceilings can, under certain circumstances, result in quantity-rationing in markets for installment credit. Usury ceilings have the effect of reducing profit margins on consumer lending operations and thus adversely affect the willingness of installment lenders to accommodate the demand for consumer credit.

The partial equilibrium analysis of the installment credit industry undertaken in Chapters 3 and 4 has laid the foundation for an analysis of the relationship between policy initiatives of the Federal Reserve System and the volume of consumer durable spending, which is the subject of Chapter 5. Chapter 5 is based on the argument that policy initiatives of the Federal Reserve Bank impact directly on consumer durable spending mainly to the extent that such initiatives exert an influence on conditions in installment credit markets.

NOTES

1. The Federal Reserve Board revised the methods by which the consumer credit statistics are calculated in 1953. Loans are classified as "industrial," "consumer" and so forth based on the type of asset(s) pledged to secure the loan. Loans to households collateralized by life insurance policies or home equity are omitted from the consumer credit statistics, even though the proceeds of such loans are often used to purchase consumer goods. For a discussion of the FED's method of calculation, see Smith *et al.* (1953), pp. 336-345.

2. Source: *Federal Reserve Bulletin*, Domestic Financial Statistics, Table 1.23.

3. The market share of commercial banks includes direct loans as well as paper purchased indirectly. Most purchases of indirect paper are purchased from retailers working through specialist dealers in installment paper. The percent of total installment paper held purchased indirectly by banks was 42% in 1986.

4. See Gilbert (1984), p. 633.

5. The geographic extent of the market for open-ended (credit card) debt is becoming increasingly national in scope. Moneycenter banks such as Citicorp have greatly expanded their credit card operations in recent years. For a discussion, see Robert E. Norton (1982), pp. 47-54.

6. For a discussion of the problem of geographic market delineation in the banking industry, see John Wolken (1984).

7. Source: *Federal Reserve Bulletin*, February 1982.

8. See Burke (1983), p. 37.

9. Heggestad and Shepard (1986), p. 309.

10. See Shepard (1982), pp. 616-617.

11. The Lerner Index (*L*) is shown as follows:

$$L = \frac{\text{Price-Marginal Cost}}{\text{Price}}$$

12. Basil Moore argues that the Federal Reserve's "support" function is more important than its "control" function, i.e., its function in controlling the quantity of bank deposits. See Moore (1978), pp. 120-138.

13. Evidence is given in Chapter 6 that the profitability of consumer lending, as measured by net earnings before taxes as a percent of installment credit outstanding, declined sharply between 1978 and 1982, a period of high short-term interest rates.

14. The idea that portfolio holders can achieve a higher rate of return for a given amount of risk through diversification is well known. Tobin put forth this idea in his seminal 1958 paper with the use of mean-variance analysis. See Tobin (1958), pp. 65-86.

15. Typically installment debt contracts call for the payment of a lump sum fee by the borrower. This fee should be included as part of the price of installment credit.

16. The classic statement of the time preference theory of the interest is by Irving Fisher. See Fisher (1911), Chapter 6. Fisher acknowledged that the concept of a perfect capital market abstracts from the problem of uncertainty and moral hazard: "Let us assume a perfect capital market in which the element of risk is entirely lacking, both with respect to the certainty of the expected income-streams belonging to different individuals, and with respect to the certainty of repayment for loans." See Fisher, *ibid.*, p. 118.

17. Defenders of the loanable funds (time preference) theory of the interest rate have insisted that the phenomena of bank credit-creation requires no essential change in their theory. For example, Dennis Robertson states: "The real value of a country's bank money is the same thing as the amount of real savings which the public has put in the past at the disposal of industry through the medium of the banks, and its amount lies in the discretion of the public and not the banks. The banks determine how much money shall be outstanding, but it is the public which determines, through the habits which it adopts as regards the hoarding and spending of money, what that amount of money shall be worth." Roberton (1940), p. 53.

18. Shackle (1967), p. 207.

19. Keynes, *op. cit.*, p. 167.

20. For a discussion of price discrimination in consumer credit markets, see Shay (1970), pp. 503-15.

21. Mandell Notes: "There are five primary functions of a credit card processing system: applications and solicitations, credit authorization, collections processing, and merchant processing. Software that will do all five functions is not widely available, and banks have had to do custom programming instead. Keeping software current is a major job, particularly for a bank that is not large enough to have a dedicated team of programmers." See Mandell (1990), p. 87.

22. See Canner and Fergus (1987), p. 2.

23. Seger (1987), p. 340.

24. For example, where credit scoring systems are used, potential borrowers are rationed when there is an increase in the minimum point score required to qualify for credit. Shay and Dunkelberg studied the effects of credit scoring systems on credit card use in New York and found that a substantial proportion of current card holders would not have qualified for card issue under tougher credit standards. See Shay and Dunkelberg (1975).

25. See Lynch (1968), pp. 592-618.

26. Conner and Fergus, *op. cit.*, p. 8.

27. See Greer, *op. cit.*, pp. 1376-1383.

28. Seeger, *op. cit.*, p. 340.

Chapter 5

Consumer Credit Expansion And Inflation

A fundamental principle which emerges from the New Quantity theory is that an increase in the rate of growth of monetary aggregates is the cause, not the effect, of inflationary pressures generated throughout the macroeconomy. The well known preference of monetarists for monetary policy "rules" is based on this principle.

Chapters 3 and 4 made the argument that in an economy in which a significant proportion of consumer expenditures are financed through access to installment credit, installment lending institutions have a vital role in sustaining the level of effective demand. Hence the rate of utilization of productive capacity depends in part on the willingness of households to incur installment liabilities on the one hand, and the willingness of financial institutions to accommodate household credit demand on the other. As was stated earlier, when installment lenders accommodate an increase in the demand for finance by the household sector there is, other things being equal, an augmentation of the economy's stock of bank money. This augmentation of the money stock is an expression of the intention of households to purchase goods and services. However, for this change in the quantity of money to be "nonneutral" in its effect on real variables means that a change in the demand for goods and services must result in an increase in the rate of flow of physical output. The concept of nonneutrality of money therefore requires an interpretation of supply-side conditions. This chapter will be restricted to a consideration of supply side conditions in durable goods industries.

The New Quantity theorists posit the existence of a "natural rate" of output and employment which is achieved as a result of optimizing behavior on the part of economic agents facing a vector of relative prices under conditions of perfect information. The natural rate of output is determined solely by "real" forces, i.e., endowments of natural resources, physical and human capital, technical know how, and the preference maps of agents with regard to the labor-leisure decision. The long run aggregate supply schedule, i.e., the schedule which is relevant under conditions of perfect information, is vertical with respect to the general price level at the natural rate of output.[1] The presumption of a "stable" demand for money function and its corollary, stable velocity of circulation, means that if the rate of growth of the nominal money stock exceeds the rate of growth the economy is capable of attaining on the basis of real forces, the increase in the quantity of money appearing on the left hand side of the equation of exchange identity must be offset to a corresponding extent by an increase in the price index appearing on its right side. This interpretation obviously suggests that money-creation as a consequence of household borrowing is a source of demand-pull inflation.[2]

The foregoing theory of inflation gained wide currency in the 1970s, culminating in a change in the Federal Reserve's operating procedure in 1979. Household borrowing in the recovery from the 1974-1975 recession was frequently cited as a contributing factor to the inflationary spiral of the late 1970s. Reinforcing this view was the fact that the ratio of installment debt liabilities outstanding to disposable personal income had risen to unprecedented levels in both 1978 and 1979 (see Figure 1-2).[3] Direct controls on consumer credit were imposed under the Credit Control Act in March, 1980.

The money-neutrality postulate of the New Quantity theory is based in part on unrealistic conception of supply side conditions prevailing in the economy. For the monetarists, the economy apparently consists of an agglomeration of atomistically structured markets in which demand conditions are revealed to economic agents through the instantaneous adjustment of relative prices. Such an economy is far removed from the real world. In the world of empirical observation, production takes time. Firms must manufacture and inventory stocks of goods in anticipation of sales which may or may not materialize. Prices are determined mainly by costs of production of which unit labor cost is often the most important element. Real world markets are never perfectly competitive, and only rarely do markets structurally approximate the competitive market model. Firms, and most importantly firms which form the core of the economy's manufacturing sector, possess a considerable degree of power over market prices.

Finally, in most real world markets for manufactured goods, changing demand conditions are not revealed through the fluid, instantaneous adjustment of relative prices, but rather through the accumulation or deaccumulation of inventory stocks of finished goods.

The present section makes the argument that, given a realistic interpretation of market structure and pricing in durable goods industries, there is a relatively limited set of circumstances under which an increase in the level of household borrowing and spending is a direct source of inflationary pressures. Moreover, it will be argued that the increase in the rate of growth of household installment borrowing in the 1975-1979 period was more the symptom of the sustained increase in the general price level as opposed to its underlying cause. Firms often meet payrolls through short term bank loans. If, owing to a negotiated increase in average hourly compensation, firms experience an increase in their wage bill, their borrowing requirements will expand commensurately. Similarly, the purchase of a given bundle of consumer durable goods by the household sector will require a greater volume of installment borrowing if the prices of those good have increased in money terms. The chain of causation therefore runs from changes in the costs of production to changes in the prices of goods and services to changes in the volume of borrowing by both firms and households. In advanced monetary economies bank money comes into existence primarily by way of loan. Thus, a change in the growth rate of the nominal money stock is in an important way an efflux of pressures emanating from the supply-side of the macroeconomy.

5.1 STRUCTURE OF DURABLE GOODS INDUSTRIES

Table 5-1 gives four-firm and eight-firm concentration ratios in selected consumer durable goods industries. The concentration ratio is defined as the percent of total value of shipments for a given industry accounted for by an absolute number of the largest domestic firms in that industry. A frequent criticism of the concentration ratio is that it fails to measure the impact on industry structure of import competition. This is a legitimate criticism inasmuch as the level of import penetration in domestic consumer goods markets has increased substantially in the past two decades. For example, the import share of the domestic auto market increased from 6.1 percent in 1965 to

25.7 percent in 1985.[4] Other areas of heavy import penetration include consumer electronics and motorcycles.

Even if import competition is taken into consideration, it is clear that consumer durable goods industries are among the most concentrated in the manufacturing sector. As measured by concentration ratios, the automobile industry is the second most concentrated domestic industry after turbogenerators. Aside from the degree of seller concentration, these industries are characterized by substantial economies of scale, product differentiation, and stiff barriers to entry.[5] A "representative" firm in consumer durable goods industries is very large both in absolute terms and with regard to its share of total market sales. Such a firm is vertically integrated, has multiplant operations, incurs heavy costs for advertising and promotion, and enjoys a significant degree of power over price. The predominant market structure in consumer durable goods industries is oligopoly. Officers of oligopolistic firms recognize fully that strategic decisions in the area of pricing, advertising, product design, or capacity expansion cannot be made without first taking into consideration the likely reaction of rival firms. Though there are many exceptions, firms in highly concentrated durable goods industries do not compete on the basis of price, preferring to adhere to an industry-wide pricing structure.[6] As a general principle, rivals in oligopolistic industries will engage in nonprice competition to increase market shares. Nonprice competition can take many forms such as frequent design modification and persuasive advertising campaigns.

Another important feature of market structure is that, under normal circumstances, a dominant firm in a durable goods industry will have substantial reserve capacity at its disposal should it decide to increase the rate of output. Based on estimates made by the Bureau of Economic Analysis, capacity utilization rates in consumer durable goods industries fluctuated between a high of 91.1% in 1966 and a low of 70.3% in 1982.[7] The element of reserve capacity is important for at least two reasons. A shift of the demand curve for consumer durables will be signaled to manufacturers through an acceleration of the rate of outflow of inventory stocks of finished goods. If inventory stocks fall below the level desired on the basis of anticipated future sales, firms ordinarily can return inventory stocks to the desired level through an increase in the rate of capacity utilization. An increase in the rate of capacity utilization will obviously expand the flow of income accruing to factors of production. The widespread existence of reserve

Table 5-1
Four-Firm and Eight-Firm Concentration Ratios in Selected Consumer Durable Goods Industries

Standard Industrial Classification (SIC) Code	Industry Definition	CR_4	CR_8
37111	Passenger Cars	99	99+
3632	Refrigerators and Freezers	82	97
3633	Laundry Equipment	83	97
36391	Water Heaters	78	98
36361	Sewing Machines	90	96
36394	Dishwashers, Disposals, and Trash Compactors	73	90
36512	Television Sets	70	93
37510	Motorcycles	NA	87
35244	Riding Lawn, Garden, and Snow Equipment	36	56
36313	Gas Ranges, Ovens, and Surface Cooking Equipment	59	82
39311	Pianos	64	90
37161	Motor Homes	39	56
36350	Vacuum Cleaners	69	88
25117	Wood Outdoor Furniture	46	66
2514	Metal Household Furniture	13	22
2515	Mattresses and Bedsprings	18	28

NA: Not Available.

Source: *Census of Manufacturers*, U. S. Department of Commerce, Subject Statistics, Volume 1, Table 9.

productive capacity under normal economic conditions explains why an expansion of purchasing power by the banking system in consequence of an increase in household borrowing invariably exerts "real" effects in the macroeconomy.

Keynes explained the persistence of excess productive capacity in western industrialized nations in terms of the insufficiency of effective demand. In contrast to the classical view as reflected by Say's Law, there exists no set of forces operating within the economy which insure that the volume of investment expenditure will be adequate to sustain full employment. The phenomena of persistent excess capacity is a troubling one for the advocates of money neutrality in so far as it is something which does not fit in an economy populated by rational economic agents. Given that the useful life of plant and equipment is measured in years or decades firms are apparently clairvoyant as to future points of effective demand when they contemplate commitments to positions in physical assets. Or, such commitments are reversible owing to the completeness of secondary markets for physical capital goods. That being the case, the phenomena of excess capacity must be traced to nominal rigidities or monetary shocks which increase information processing problems for economic agents. The New Classical economists view factors such as uncertainty, imperfect competition, and sunk costs as microeconomic frictions. Such frictions should be abstracted from in formal models for reasons of mathematical tractability or in the interest of maintaining continuity with received doctrine. However, what the New Classical economists regard as frictions are in fact essential features of real world industrial economies. To abstract from these elements is to greatly obscure the relationship between money and economic activity.

Discussion of the factors which determine price formation in durable goods industries is relevant in the context of the thesis to the extent that it should shed light on the relationship, if any, between household borrowing, installment lending, and the prices of consumer durable goods. The inflationary effect of household borrowing can be easily demonstrated in the framework for partial equilibrium analysis. For example, suppose there is a "composite" durable good. If, other things being equal, the household sector desires to increase its expenditures for the composite durable, and if this demand is made effective through the accommodation of additional borrowing requirements by installment lenders, then this will be represented by a outward shift of the market demand schedule. The market supply schedule is given by the horizontal summation of short run marginal cost functions of firms supplying the durable good. Consistent with the law of diminishing returns, firms are assumed to experience rising marginal cost in the "relevant range" of output. Hence, the market supply schedule has a positive slope. A shift of the demand curve will therefore result in a higher equilibrium price. Assuming our durable good is weighted in the calculation of a composite price index, the increase in spending made possible by access to finance is clearly a source of inflation. Household borrowing results in demand-pull (diminishing returns) inflation. This conclusion derives from a particular interpretation of the supply schedule in durable goods industries. But does the above interpretation represent a fair approximation of actual cost conditions in durable goods industries?

5.2 PRICE FORMATION IN DURABLE GOODS INDUSTRIES

The previous section described some salient structural characteristics of domestic durable goods industries. Most of these industries exhibit a high degree of seller concentration. As is perhaps the most important feature of oligopolistic market structures, sellers are interdependent. And such interdependence is in most all cases recognized by rival firms. The problem of price formation in consumer durable goods industries is therefore best approached in the framework of cost-plus pricing models. The present section will draw heavily on the work of Alfred Eichner in this area. Specifically, Eichner's model of pricing in oligopolistic industries with "dominant firm" price leadership is set forth.

The basic principle underlying cost-plus pricing models is as follows: In concentrated market structures with significant barriers-to-entry, market prices are "administered" by firms based on a mark-up over unit costs of production. Supply schedules are highly elastic at administered prices reflecting the relative constancy of unit prime costs over a wide range of capacity utilization rates. The question of what factors govern the mark-up over average unit cost has been the subject of considerable controversy. For Kalecki, it was the much criticized "degree of monopoly."[8] Eichner approached this issue in more rigorous fashion, bringing to bear on the problem the tools of Industrial Organization analysis and especially the contributions of Joe Bain the area of limit-pricing theory.[9]

Eichner regarded his theory as novel in the sense that the pricing decision of the dominant firm (or megacorp) was taken to be fundamentally related to the firm's desired rate of capital formation.[10]

The mark-up over unit cost, or what Eichner termed the "corporate levy," is determined based on the desired flow of internally generated investment funds:

> It follows that any change in price will necessarily reflect a change in one of the pricing formula's components. Assuming variable and fixed costs remain constant, the change in price will, then, be due to a change in the required corporate levy. Any change in the corporate levy will, in turn, depend on the megacorp's demand for and supply cost of internally generated investment funds. Thus, the pricing decision in an oligopolistic industry is intimately bound up with the capital accumulation process.[11]

In Eichner's model, industry-wide prices are set by the megacorp-price leader. The institution of price leadership evolves out of the recognition of interdependence among rival firms as well as the need to avoid ruinous price wars. This need is particularly acute where fixed costs are substantial in relation to total operating costs. Formally, the model is presented as follows:

$$P = AVC + \frac{FC + CL}{SOR \ x \ ERC}$$

where P = absolute price level

AVC = average variable costs

FC = fixed costs

CL = corporate levy

SOR = standard operating ratio

ERC = engineer-rated capacity

A few points need further discussion here. Average variable cost takes its usual meaning. Variable costs can change due to a change in the price of labor or materials. With a given production technique and fixed technical coefficients, average variable costs cannot change due to a change in relative factor intensities. Eichner put research and development costs, advertising and promotion expenses, and dividend payments to equity holders in the category of fixed cost. Hence the realized corporate levy will accrue as retained earnings.

The term ERC is defined as:

> [The] sum of capacities of all plants or plant segments, these capacities in turn being specified as the quantities which, in the judgment of the engineers who designed them, each of the plant or plant segments owned by the megacorp is capable of producing when operating at maximum efficiency. It corresponds to the level of output at which, all plants having been put into operation, marginal costs begin to rise sharply and continuously.[12]

The standard operating ratio (SOR) is

> [The] percentage of total capacity at which, based on past experience, the megacorp can expect to operate on the average over the business cycle. It takes into account the fact that the megacorp will already have sufficient reserve capacity to meet any likely fluctuations in demand.[13]

The denominator of equation (1) gives the level of output the oligopolistic firm is likely to produce at a given point in time based on forecasts of short-term demand conditions. If, for example, the SOR is 80%, then the firm can increase its capacity utilization rate by a substantial degree while maintaining constant average variable (prime) costs. This point is important because it means that, under normal circumstances, aggregate demand for consumer durable goods could expand by a significant amount without generating diminishing returns inflation. Hence, in Eichner's model, prices are supply-determined and quantities are demand-determined.

The ex ante per unit corporate levy is determined by the firm's desired flow of internally generated investment funds. The realized corporate levy is an ex post phenomena, i.e., it depends upon total sales volume. If demand forecasts are accurate, then the firm will realize a flow of retained earnings consistent with its investment plans. What factors place an upper limit on the per unit corporate levy or on industry prices generally? Eichner listed three factors: (1) The substitution effect; (2) the entry factor, and; (3) the possibility of meaningful government intervention. The first factor depends on the availability of substitutes or cross-price elasticity relationships. With respect to the second factor, firms in oligopolistic industries enjoy market power because potential entrants suffer disadvantages in comparison with incumbent firms. Disadvantages suffered by potential entrants, defined by Bain as barriers-to-entry, can take many forms. Bain defined three types: (1) Barriers due to economies of scale; (2) barriers due to absolute cost advantages, and; (3) barriers due to product differentiation.[14] Incumbent firms will have a strong incentive to price their products at a level below that which would induce entry of new firms into the industry. Ordinarily, firms will not price their product above Bain's "maximum entry-forestalling price."[15] This element constitutes a limiting factor on the size of per unit corporate levy.

The threat of government intervention also enters into the determination of the mark-up. Excessive profits might result in price regulation, antitrust prosecution, or other government responses. The excess profits tax imposed on the domestic petroleum industry during the Carter Administration is a recent example.

A graphical presentation of Eichner's model is given in Figure 5-1.

Figure 5-1

Pricing in Durable Goods Industries

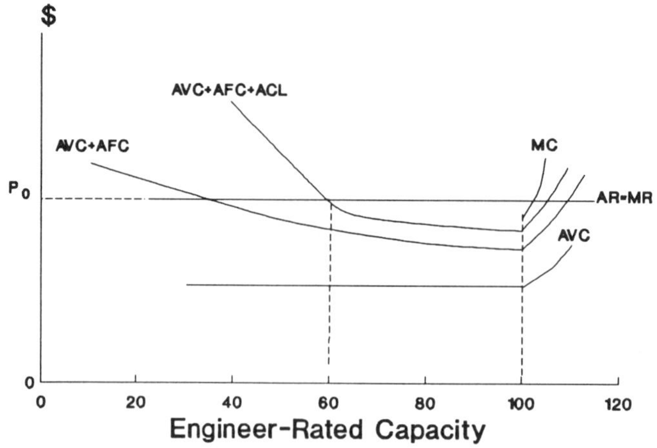

Source: Alfred Eichner, *The Megacorp and Oligopoly.*

The standard operating ratio is assumed to be 60%. Based on the required corporate levy and other elements of the pricing formula, the firm sets a price of P_0 and stands ready to supply what the market will bear at that price. Note that diminishing returns does not set in until the capacity utilization rate exceeds 100% of engineer-rated capacity. The BEA estimates of capacity utilization in durable goods industries indicate that capacity utilization rates fluctuate between about 90% at the peak of the business cycle and about 70% at the trough. As capacity utilization rates increase, firms could experience rising unit prime costs for two reasons. The first reason would be diminishing returns as represented by a continuous, positively sloped marginal cost schedule. An alternative explanation would be that as the rate of output increases there is pressure exerted on the prices of materials and labor. This would be represented by a broken, or discontinuous, marginal cost schedule. Though the principle of diminishing returns is conceptually appealing when applied to the problem of agricultural production, it makes a less than smooth transition to the realm of heavy manufacturing. Specifically, it is very difficult to accept the proposition that diminishing returns is relevant in normal conditions when reserve capacity is the rule and not the exception. It follows that an increase in aggregate demand for consumer durable goods will not generate inflationary pressures due to diminishing returns except under highly unusual circumstances.

5.3 SUMMARY

The foregoing argument should not be taken to suggest that the volume of consumer durable spending has no relationship whatsoever to the general price level. The volume of durable spending can contribute indirectly to spot price inflation by virtue of derived demand relationships. Many primary commodities are traded in spot markets which fit the general description of Hicksean "flex price" markets. In these spot markets trading occurs within the Marshallian market period, meaning that available stocks of commodities cannot be adjusted in response to changing market conditions. Thus a change in demand is manifest solely in the adjustment of the spot price. As an example, the spot price of bauxite ore is strongly influenced by worldwide demand for aluminum. The demand for aluminum depends in part on the demand for automobiles since autos contain many aluminum parts. Hence by virtue of derived demand, an increase in the demand for autos can exert upward pressure on the spot price of bauxite ore. This in turn would be reflected by an upward shift of car manufacturers marginal and average variable cost schedules. Given our cost plus pricing formula, the change in production costs must lead to higher car prices. The change would not be immediate, however, since an increase in the spot price of commodities does not affect the costs of production for cars already manufactured and inventoried.

A more complicated issue concerns the relationship between aggregate demand and the price of labor. The wage bill is typically the most important element of prime cost in durable goods industries. For the most part, workers in durable goods industries are unionized and their compensation is set as part of the terms of collective bargaining agreements. The labor market is not a spot market and wage rates tend to be sticky. If organized labor is successful in negotiating increases in money compensation, and if the growth rate of money wages exceeds gains made in labor productivity, then the price of durable goods must increase due to higher unit labor costs. This phenomena is referred to as incomes inflation. It is a common observation that labor finds its position strengthened and exhibits greater truculence when the general level of business activity is comparatively high. Thus, an increase in aggregate demand might contribute to incomes inflation in a very indirect way if labor is able to exploit the situation and gain wage increases.

Notes

1. It could be stated alternatively that the long run Phillips curve is vertical at the "natural rate" of unemployment. See Friedman (1968), pp. 1-17.

2. Again, this result is based on the assumption of complete information. Or more specifically, the information set possessed by agents is assumed to be sufficient to disentangle relative price movements from movements in the general price level. In Rational Expectations formulations of the Natural Rate hypothesis, complete information allows economic agents to "fully anticipate" changes in the rate of growth of the nominal money stock. See Barro and Rush (1980), and Mishkin (1982).

3. Total household debt outstanding--including mortgage debt, installment and noninstallment credit and other loans--expanded by one third between 1975 and 1977. Mortgage debt alone increased by nearly 35 billion dollars in the same period. Seiders and Luckett argued that most of this increase could be explained by the fact that the median selling price of existing homes doubled between 1970-1977. See Sediers and Luckett (1978), pp. 157-159.

4. Source: *Ward's Automotive Yearbook.*

5. Scherer, Beckenstein, Kaufer, and Murphy estimated minimum efficient scale as a percent of U.S. 1967 output to evaluate the importance of scale economies in manufacturing industries. They concluded that the pursuit of scale economies was sufficient to explain the high degree of seller concentration in numerous durable goods industries, including autos, refrigerators, and laundry equipment. See Scherer, *et al.* (1975).

6. The automotive industry is usually given as the classic example of "dominant firm" price leadership, with General Motors acting as price leader. For a discussion of price leadership in the automotive industry, see Markham (1951), pp. 891-905 and Kahn (1959), pp. 670-578.

7. The BEA measure of capacity utilization is "survey-based." Respondents at the plant level are asked to estimate "practical capacity" based on the maximum number of shifts per day "consistent with a realistic work pattern." The difference between "actual" capacity utilization and practical capacity then gives the capacity utilization rate.

It should be noted that respondents are instructed not to consider overtime pay, added costs for materials, or other costs to be limiting factors in setting capacity. For a description of the BEA measure and other measures of capacity utilization, see Frank de Leeuw (1979), pp. 45-55.

8. A frequent criticism of Kalecki's model is that his "degree of monopoly" is a tautological concept. Kalecki defined the degree of monopoly as: $X = P - MC/P$, where P is unit price Kalecki's degree of monopoly is therefore identical to the Lerner measure of monopoly. See Kalecki (1939), p. 43.

9. See Bain (1968), pp. 302-386.

10. See Eichner (1982), pp. 9-10.

11. *Ibid.*, p. 56.

12. *Ibid.*, p. 62.

13. *Ibid.*, p. 62.

14. Bain (1968), pp. 255-256.

15. *Ibid.*, p. 259.

Chapter 6

Federal Reserve Policy and Consumer Spending: The Linkages

This chapter will examine the relationship between the use of discretionary policy by the Federal Reserve System and changes in the volume of expenditure for consumer durable goods. Policy initiatives of the Federal Reserve Bank (hereafter referred to as the FED) can, in principal at least, act to stimulate or attenuate the level of consumer durable spending by virtue of both direct and indirect effects which tend to be mutually reinforcing. For example, if FED policies are effective in influencing the general level of business activity, this will affect the volume of consumer spending indirectly through a change in the flow of the income accruing to households. The subject of indirect effects as operating through changes in the volume of aggregate income is not the subject of this volume. Rather the focus is placed on direct effects which are defined as those effects of FED policy which impinge directly on conditions in installment credit markets.

In Chapter 3 consumer spending was divided into two categories termed C_1 and C_2. C_2 was defined as that proportion of total consumer spending which is determined by factors other than the volume of current income. C_2 was in turn posited to be strongly influenced by the following variables: (1) The attitude of the household sector toward debt obligations, and (2) the ability and/or willingness of commercial banks, finance companies, and other installment lenders to accommodate the demand for finance by the household sector. The first factor shapes the demand schedule for consumer installment credit while the latter shapes the supply schedule. Building upon the partial equilibrium framework developed in Chapters 3 and 4, the present chapter will specify and discuss the various mechanisms by which alternative policy initiatives of the FED are manifest in changing demand or supply side conditions in installment credit markets.

The outline of the present chapter is as follows. Section 6.1 will discuss the rules and requirements pertaining to the eligibility for discount of consumer installment paper under the Federal Reserves Regulation A. This topic is included because the conditions under which the FED is prepared to exercise its "lender of last resort" function can have important implications with respect to bank lending practices. That is to say that the regulations pertaining to the eligibility for discount of different types of bank assets render such assets more or less liquid and hence are capable of influencing the desired composition of bank portfolios. The Credit Control Act of 1969 is the subject of section 6.2. Section 6.3 concerns the direct regulation by the FED of hire-purchase terms stipulated in installment debt contracts such as the minimum required down payment, length to maturity, or minimum collateral requirements. Section 6.4 presents an interpretation of the transmission mechanism connecting changes in the conduct of open market operations by the FED and changes in the volume of spending for consumer durable goods. The interpretation set forth in section 6.4 stands in contrast to well-known interpretations of the transmission mechanism based on net wealth or portfolio adjustment effects. Section 6.5 explores the effects on consumer durable spending of direct credit controls imposed under the Credit Control Act as well as the conduct of open market operations during the 1979-1982 recession, a period during which the FED was widely perceived to have pursued a "contractionary" monetary policy.

6.1 THE FEDERAL RESERVE ACT AND REGULATION A

It was stated in Chapter 4 that consumer installment paper is held by various installment lenders because it is a source of income. For commercial banks installment receivables constitute a part of the portfolio of earning assets. But it is also true that, as a general principle, given a choice among assets which are similar in all respects save for the degree of liquidity attached to them, lenders will prefer the asset which offers the highest degree of liquidity. In enumerating the factors which condition the willingness of lenders to hold installment paper, one factor given was "the degree of liquidity attached to installment paper, or the assessment on the part of lenders as to the future possibility of discounting consumer installment paper in secondary markets or at the FED discount window." Given the preference of lenders for assets which combine high expected yields with liquidity, the existence of an institution which acts as "buyer of last resort" in the secondary market for consumer installment paper would, other things being equal, tend to facilitate a continuous flow of credit extensions to the household sector by making installment paper a more attractive asset in the view of lenders.[1] As was stated in Chapter 4, the secondary market for consumer installment receivables does not compare in a structural sense with markets for other financial assets such as equities or Treasury issues. Therefore, there is a much greater degree of uncertainty attached to the future spot price and liquidity of installment paper as compared to alternative assets which commercial banks are legally permitted to hold in their portfolios. Hence the terms on which the FED is prepared to perform the "buyer of last resort" function is capable of influencing the composition of bank portfolios and the ability of commercial, industrial and household borrowers to obtain credit.

The Federal Reserve Act of 1913 reflected an explicit recognition on the part of politicians and other policy makers of the central banks function as "lender of last resort." Under the reorganization of the national banking system in 1913 the Federal Reserve Bank stood ready to provide for "elasticity of reserves" to the banking system in accord with the requirements of commerce. Jane Knodell has described the system as follows:

> Banker's dissatisfaction with the reserve system, together with the changing orientation of the Federal Government toward the economy, culminated in the Federal Reserve Act of 1913. This Act created a mechanism for the supply of reserves to the banking

> system in a manner responsive to fluctuation in the banking system's need for reserves--the discount window. Banks could get reserves either by borrowing on the collateral of eligible paper, or by discounting eligible paper (commercial paper and trade acceptances) with the reserve bank, at an administered discount rate. Reserve banks were essentially buyers of last resort of bank holdings of short-term paper, rendering the demand for this paper perfectly elastic at the stated discount rate. The creation of a central discounting facility dramatically transformed the operating environment of commercial banks by regularizing the supply of reserves to the banking system. This allowed banks to regard their loan portfolios as sources of profits over the long term and not as sources of liquidity over the short term.[2]

If, as Knodell argues, the Federal Reserve Act resulted in an increasing preference by bankers for income-earning, less liquid assets in their portfolios, then the system must have worked in favor of the growth and maturity of consumer credit markets. This follows from the fact the installment paper is held primarily because it is a source of profit.

As was pointed out above, an important method by which the FED exercises its lender of last resort function is through the discounting of commercial bank assets or the acceptance of bank assets as security against advances made to banks by the Federal Reserve. The Congress and Federal Reserve officials are in a position to influence, to some degree, the lending practices of commercial banks by setting forth guidelines concerning the eligibility of bank assets for discount or for their eligibility as collateral against FED advances.[3] With respect to the willingness of commercial banks to accommodate household credit demand, bankers are likely to have a more favorable attitude toward consumer installment paper if such paper is eligible under the guidelines set forth in Regulation A.

Under the unrevised version of Regulation A, only paper classified as "self-liquidating" is eligible for discount or as security against FED advances. The term "self-liquidating" paper refers mainly to short term industrial and commercial loans which are made for the purpose of procuring inventory stocks of intermediate or finished commodities or for meeting payrolls. Such loans were viewed as self-liquidating in the sense that they would be repaid in a relatively short period of time through the sale of goods and services. Hence, assets eligible under Regulation A were generally loans made for the purchase of circulating capital.

Consumer installment paper was not eligible under the unrevised version of Regulation A. Regulation A was revised effective October 1, 1937. It states that, "when in judgment of the Federal Reserve Bank circumstances made it advisable to do so, the bank may accept as security for such advances any assets satisfactory to it." Included among these were "obligations which are issued or drawn for the purposes of financing or refinancing the sale of goods on an installment basis."[4] The eligibility of installment paper, which includes paper held by finance companies, is subject to provisos that it is "sound" paper and its maturity does not exceed 90 days. The latter proviso is important in that the majority of installment paper held by financial institutions will have a maturity exceeding 90 days and thus is not eligible under subsection D.

What factors led to a revision of Regulation A? On one level it was part of a flurry of new legislation (including deposit insurance and the Glass-Steagall Act) enacted in response to the banking crisis of the 1930s. However, there was also been a growing awareness of the importance of installment lending institutions in maintaining a wide and deep market for consumer durable goods. As is well known spending for consumer durable goods declined precipitously between 1929 and 1933. What is less well known is that exposure to installment paper by banks and finance companies dropped sharply in the same period. In October, 1929, installment credit outstanding was equal to $3.17 billion, a decline of 66% in nominal terms from the pre-Depression high.[5] Keynesian scholars generally attribute the durable goods slump of the Great Depression to a set of demand-side causes including falling personal income, a decline in personal wealth resulting from the stock market crash and deteriorating consumer confidence.[6] Another element may have worked in combination with these factors to produce the slump in durable spending. In a period of recurring liquidity crises within the banking system, bank officers will have a tendency to reorganize portfolios in favor of short-term liquid assets which offer a greater degree of certainty with regard to their future spot price and liquidity. Epstein and Ferguson state, for example:

> By the middle of the Great Contraction, bank portfolios in many federal reserve districts were beginning to assume a curious shape. Either because bankers were becoming very wary or because good lending opportunities were difficult to find, loans were falling off

> catastrophically. The loan liquidation effect then took hold. As loans and many bonds became increasingly risky, bankers looked around for ways to maintain earnings. In due course, they began to purchase larger and larger amounts of the safest asset that remained available in large quantities--short term government securities. Whereas in 1929 investments made up less than 30 percent of member bank earning asset portfolios, by the end of 1933 they made up almost 50 percent. A large percentage of the increase took the form of increases in the holdings of government securities.[7]

Prior to 1937, there was no "buyer of last resort" in the market for installment credit. Hence, bankers may have been reluctant to layer their portfolios with installment receivables for fear that these assets could not be discounted at a later date to meet a reserve deficiency. The revisions to Regulation A probably attenuated this fear by establishing the FED as buyer of last resort in the secondary market for installment paper.

A case can be made for the further liberalization of Regulation A guidelines pertaining to FED discount of installment paper. The volume of spending by households for consumer durable good depends upon, among other things, households being able to obtain the credit necessary to execute buying plans. A general "flight to liquidity" on the part of commercial lenders will obviously result in a curtailment of installment extensions to households and consequent contraction of aggregate demand. The FED is in a position to counteract such a development by giving assurances that it will maintain the liquidity of installment paper should a crisis develop.

6.2 THE CREDIT CONTROL ACT OF 1969

Under the Credit Control Act of 1969 the Federal Reserve Board can be authorized to control and regulate extensions of credit by member commercial banks if the President "determines such action is necessary for the purpose of controlling inflation generated by the extension of credit in excessive volume." A Presidential authorization may specify particular categories of loans, e.g., industrial, commercial, loans to brokers, mortgage loans, revolving credit of households, etc., or it may be a request by the President for general limitations on credit expansion. In either case, the Federal Reserve board has wide discretion with respect to the specific means by which controls are implemented under a Presidential authorization. These include the direct regulation of interest rates and/or nonprice terms of credit contracts. Also, the FED maintains power over the licensing of lending institutions. Hence, the FED may exert considerable control over both the direction and volume of credit expansion by virtue of its power to issue or revoke lending licenses. It should be noted that the power to revoke licenses is infrequently exercised in practice. Another means by which the FED can implement credit controls is by setting maximum loan-to-deposit or loan-to-asset ratios for creditors or debtors.

Consumer installment credit has been a target of direct credit controls on one occasion since the passage of the Credit Control Act of 1969. President Carter, citing the build-up of household indebtedness as a contributing factor to both inflationary pressures and, historically, a relatively low savings rate on the part of domestic households during the recovery from the 1973-1975 recession, invoked his authority under the Credit Control Act on March 14, 1980. Executive Order 12201 stated the following:

> . . . each covered creditor shall hold a non-interest bearing deposit equal to 15% of the amount by which the average amount of its covered credit outstanding during the calendar month exceeds its base.

"Covered" creditors meant all suppliers of consumer credit with a least 2 million dollars of consumer debt appearing as "accounts receivable" on their accounting statements as of March 14, 1980. Under this definition, the majority of commercial banks and consumer finance companies were covered under the executive order. The extent to which retail establishments such as major department stores and appliance retail business were covered by the credit controls is difficult to ascertain. Though a significant proportion of consumer credit extensions originate at "the point of sale," installment contracts offered by retailers are generally presented to finance companies or commercial banks for discount.[8] Thus, in a given year a particular retail establishment may offer point-of-sale credit extensions well in excess of $2 million dollars; yet, at the end of the year the value of consumer installment receivables might be substantially less than $2 million owing to the discount of such paper. Hence, this establishment would not be "covered" since the guidelines are based on the stock of credit outstanding and not the volume of extensions granted in a particular time interval. Table 6-1 shows the volume of extensions of point-of-sale credit (in millions) by retailers and the percent of installment paper outstanding held by retail establishments in selected years. Data for more recent years is unavailable since the Federal Reserve discontinued publication of the repayments and extensions series in 1982. However, the data seem to be consistent with the view that at least some of the large regional or national-based retail chains were in the category of "covered" creditors during the imposition of direct controls from March, 1980, through January, 1981. Installment paper held by retailers amounted to nearly 3 billion in 1981. To get a more accurate picture one would need to know the distribution of installment holding as among the greater than 10,000 retail enterprises which offer point-of-sale credit in the United States.

The FED defined "covered" credit to include all consumer installment debt except loans collateralized by automobiles, mobile homes, and appliances. It is clear on the basis of public statements as well as the wording of Executive Order 12201 that President Carter's main objective was to restrain the growth of credit card extensions or extensions made on revolving account, as they are defined in the consumer credit statistics. There is, unfortunately, considerable ambiguity as to the proportion of total extensions made on credit card accounts which ought to be properly regarded as consumer loans. Households will usually have the option of avoiding interest charges if they pay off their credit card balances in full during the grace period. The relevant question is what proportion of consumer debt outstanding on revolving account is typically paid off within, say, 30 days. This is a particularly important question since the growth rate of revolving credit outstanding has exceeded the growth rate of installment extensions of all types of consumer credit in some years. Indeed, revolving credit has been the fastest growing component of installment debt since 1983. In 1984-1985 revolving credit increased by 26%, compared to 20% for automobile credit and 20% for all other types of consumer credit. Table 6-2 gives quarterly data indicating the growth rates of credit card debt outstanding, total installment debt outstanding, and debt outstanding on revolving accounts as a percent of total installment debt.

Table 6-1

Extensions of Installment Credit and Installment Debt Outstanding Held by Retailers

Year	Extensions by Retailers (millions of current dollars)	Percent of Total Extensions	Installment Debt Outstanding Held by Retailers[1] (millions of current dollars)	Percent of Total
1976	29,447	13.9	19,260	9.9
1977	39,133	15.4	23,490	10.1
1978	41,619	13.9	24,876	9.0
1979	46,092	14.2	27,916	8.9
1980	50,959	16.6	29,410	9.4
1981	53,430	15.8	29,551	8.6

[1]Amount outstanding in December of each year.

Source: *Federal Reserve Bulletin, Domestic Financial Statistics*, Tables 1.56 and 1.57.

As Table 6-2 reveals, household borrowing was very strong in 1977 and 1978. Debt outstanding on revolving accounts as a percent of total outstanding installment credit increased by 87% between the first quarter of 1975 and the fourth quarter of 1979. Hence, borrowing on credit card accounts drove the growth rate of total installment debt outstanding to an increasing extent throughout the period, the exceptions being the first quarter of 1978.[9]

As indicated earlier, the consumer debt figures may, however, be overstated in so far as they include convenience use of credit card accounts. Luckett and August adjusted the consumer debt figures for convenience use by assuming that about one-half of the debt outstanding on charge accounts was owed by "revolving users" and hence ought to be considered as consumer debt, and that the other half was owed by "convenience users" and should be omitted from the statistics on consumer debt. The assumption concerning the division of credit card debt between "convenience use" and "revolving use" was based on the results of FED-sponsored "Survey of Consumer Finances" published in 1967 and 1983. The estimates of Luckett and August are shown in Table 6-3. As can be seen by Table 6-3, the convenience-adjusted figures are systematically lower than the actual growth rate of installment debt outstanding in the period indicated.

The effects of the direct credit controls imposed in 1980 on the volume of installment credit extensions and consumer durable spending will be discussed in section 5.6. A few points may be raised here concerning the general desirability and effectiveness of direct controls on consumer credit. With regard to the desirability of direct controls, the important question is: What purpose are credit controls ostensibly designed to serve? That President Carter's main objective in invoking the Act was to attenuate the inflationary spiral of the late 1970s should not be doubted. Might direct controls be purposefully used in the pursuit of other policy objectives? In principle, direct controls might be deployed in an effort to reshape commercial bank portfolios in favor of assets which are comparatively less risky from an actuarial standpoint. The benefits of such controls would presumably derive from fewer bank insolvencies and reduced pressure on the Federal Deposit Insurance Corporation Fund. As was pointed out in Chapter 4, consumer installment loans are not a particularly risky proposition for commercial banks. Consumer lending offers a means by which banks can diversify their portfolios of earnings assets. Also, with the

Table 6-2

Growth of Consumer Installment Debt, Credit Card Debt, and the Ratio of Revolving Debt to Total Consumer Installment Debt Outstanding

Year and Quarter		Annual Rate of Growth in Outstanding Debt (Percent): Total Installment Debt	Annual Rate of Growth in Outstanding Debt (Percent): On Revolving Accounts	Debt Outstanding on Revolving Accounts as a Percent of Total Installment Debt
1975:	1....	4.1	18.3	4.9
	2....	1.9	13.2	5.0
	3....	2.1	10.1	5.2
	4....	4.5	10.1	5.4
1976:	1....	7.3	16.8	5.3
	2....	10.4	18.9	5.2
	3....	11.5	20.6	5.5
	4....	12.5	21.9	5.9
1977:	1....	18.1	16.1	5.4
	2....	17.6	21.3	5.6
	3....	15.6	24.6	5.9
	4....	17.5	28.7	6.3
1978:	1....	16.7	-.8	6.0
	2....	20.8	42.3	8.2
	3....	16.0	35.7	8.6
	4....	15.8	21.4	9.2
1979:	1....	17.5	21.3	8.8
	2....	13.7	27.4	8.9
	3....	13.2	25.1	9.2
	4....	10.4	14.5	9.2

Source: *Business Conditions Digest*, Series 66 and the *Federal Reserve Bulletin*, Domestic Financial Statistics, A46, Table 1.56.

exception of loans on revolving accounts, installment loans are typically collateralized by consumer durable goods. Charge-offs are regarded as a normal cost of making installment extensions, and this cost is reflected in the higher interest charges households pay on average relative to commercial and industrial borrowers. In summary, a convincing argument for credit controls on the ground of limiting the riskiness of bank portfolios is difficult to make.

An argument can be made, however, for the use of selective credit controls to smooth the growth rate of installment debt outstanding. Holding the average maturity of installment debt contracts and the growth of installment debt outstanding means that a larger fraction of disposable income in succeeding months and quarters will be claimed by debt servicing. Hence, the stock of household debt constitutes a near-term constraint on household spending. The use of direct controls to prevent a sudden build-up of consumer debt thus may serve to stabilize aggregate expenditure by limiting the extent to which debt servicing claims purchasing power from current income. As was discussed in Chapter 3, durable spending is influenced by the household attitude toward debt obligations. A rapid accumulation of debt on household balance sheets can set the stage for an episode of household debt deflation if it contributes to a general aversion on the part of households to additional debt liabilities. Hence the use of direct controls to target the growth rate of installment extensions might be helpful in stabilizing the level of consumer spending by reducing the risk of debt deflation.

The use of direct controls as an anti-inflation weapon is obviously based on the assumption that household borrowing is a contributing factor to inflation. Is this a tenable assumption? The relationship between installment borrowing, consumer durable spending, and the average prices of durable goods is the subject of the Chapter 5.

Are direct credit controls effective in restraining the volume of installment borrowing and lending? The Federal Reserve Board is on record in opposition to the direct regulation of credit extensions of any type. In fact, FED officials have argued in favor of the repeal or modification of the Credit Control Act of 1969. The FED's opposition appears to be based on two arguments. First, credit controls don't work. Second, direct controls interfere with the efficient operation of financial markets.

Table 6-3

Convenience Adjusted Rate of Growth of Consumer Installment Credit

Year and Quarter		Annual Rate of Growth in Outstanding Debt	
		Actual	Convenience Adjusted[1]
1977:	1....	18.1	18.5
	2....	17.6	16.3
	3....	15.6	15.6
	4....	17.5	15.9
1978:	1....	16.7	16.0
	2....	20.8	19.8
	3....	16.0	14.8
	4....	15.8	15.1
1979:	1....	17.5	16.0
	2....	13.7	12.2
	3....	13.2	12.0
	4....	10.4	9.5
1980:	1....	7.4	8.3
	2....	-8.3	-9.7
	3....	(2)	(2)
	4....	2.2	1.8
1981:	1....	6.9	6.3
	2....	6.9	5.9
	3....	7.8	7.6
	4....	.4	.1
1982:	1....	5.0	4.5
	2....	6.5	5.8
	3....	2.8	2.5
	4....	5.0	4.9
1983:	1....	8.6	8.0
	2....	11.6	10.6
	3....	14.7	14.4
	4....	20.4	19.2
1984:	1....	18.5	17.4
	2....	23.4	22.0
	3....	16.8	16.3
	4....	17.1	16.3

[1]"Convenience-adjusted" debt is actual debt minus cumulative growth in convenience credit.

Source: Luckett and August (1985), p. 398.

Nancy Teeters of the Board of Governors outlined this view as follows:

> The nature of financial markets in this country makes credit controls both unneeded--save for very exceptional circumstances--and extremely difficult to administer. Our credit markets reflect the borrowing and lending decisions of vast numbers of consumers and businesses and are an important means through which our economic resources are efficiently allocated among competing uses. The market is so large and fluid that credit is generally available to all qualified borrowers, though the price--that is, interest rate--will vary as to ration the supplies o funds.
>
> Imposition of controls in such a free, well-functioning market inevitably invokes a response by market participants, who attempt to circumvent the controls. Lenders seek the most profitable outlets for their funds, whether at home or abroad. And borrowers, who may be blocked out of one market, may seek funds in another. The fungibility of money and credit makes it most difficult to administer credit controls selectively, and enhances the likelihood that one set of controls will only give rise to another.[10]

Teeters did not mention the efficacy of hire-purchase restrictions on installment debt contracts in her policy statement. The use of hire-purchase controls to target the volume of consumer credit lending is the subject of section 6.3.

6.3 THE REGULATION OF HIRE-PURCHASE TERMS

The direct regulation of hire-purchase terms is one practical way by which the FED can target the flow of installment credit extensions forthcoming from both the commercial banking system and nonbank financial institutions. The hire-purchase, or nonprice, terms stipulated in installment debt contracts constitute a very important element in the household decision to borrow. Nonprice terms include the minimum required downpayment, maximum length top maturity, as well as specific collateralization requirements. As was stated in Chapter 3, the purchase of consumer credit serves to alleviate a cash flow problem which ordinarily arises in the procurement of big-ticket durable goods. It is for this reason that nonprice credit terms may often weigh more heavily in the judgment of household borrowers than the actual price of credit as expressed by the average percentage rate. Thus it will often be the case that borrowers will be willing to pay a higher price for credit if they can obtain more liberal nonprice credit terms. The liberalization of hire-purchase terms will typically increase the total amount paid by the consumer over the life of the installment contract; however, the allocation of weekly or monthly household income to debt servicing will not be as large as would be the case under more stringent nonprice terms. A reason frequently given for the rapid build-up of household indebtedness after the Korean War was the general liberalization of hire-purchase terms on installment debt contracts. Particularly important was the introduction of the 24 month auto loan.[11]

Within the framework of the partial equilibrium model of the installment credit market developed in Chapter 4, the direct manipulation of hire-purchase terms by the FED has the effect of shifting the household demand curve for finance. Along a demand schedule derived with respect to the price of credit, the set of nonprice terms attached to installment contracts is held constant. A change in hire-purchase terms can be expected to shift the demand curve for finance because a change in the minimum downpayment or in the maximum repayment period will have the effect of exerting more or less pressure on the short-term budget constraint for a loan of a given amount. The effectiveness of hire-purchase regulations in stimulating or attenuating the volume of household borrowing clearly depends on the magnitude of the shift in demand for finance.

As was pointed out in the previous section, Federal Reserve officials have stated that direct credit controls are ineffectual in accomplishing their stated purpose and produce frictions in credit markets as an unintended side effect. This argument cannot be made uncategorically with regard to hire-purchase controls since the record on this count is extremely limited. Direct regulations on hire-purchase terms have been imposed on only two occasions in the United States. Controls were imposed by the FED from 1942-1945 and again from 1948-1952. The controls were imposed during the Korean War because it was feared that the public, with the experience of the World War II shortages fresh in their memory, might resort to a flurry of panic buying. The controls of the 1948-1952 period required a minimum downpayment on durable purchases of 20% and limited maturities on installment debt contracts to twelve months.

As was discussed in Chapter 2, the best known empirical study of the effects of Korean War controls on consumer spending was done by

Hamburger and Zwick.[12] As is the case in many empirical studies of consumer durable spending, Hamburger and Zwick used the stock adjustment model, which supposes that households have a "desired" stock of consumer durables and an "actual" stock and then attempt, through spending for durables, to eliminate some fraction of the difference between the desired and actual stock each quarter. The hire-purchase variable specified as an independent variable generated modest explanatory power. The use of hire-purchase controls to moderate spending has been a more frequent practice in the United Kingdom. The Report of the Committee on the *Working of the Monetary System*,[13] more commonly known as the Radcliffe Report, noted that "the controls of hire purchase terms have had a sizeable impact, of a once-and-for-all kind, on each major change," but that "these sizeable effects on total demand have implied major directional effects which, though sometimes deliberately sought, have in general been detrimental to industrial efficiency."[14] Chapter 2, section 2.4 reviewed the empirical literature pertaining to the British experience with hire-purchase controls on installment debt contracts.

6.4 OPEN MARKET OPERATIONS AND CONSUMER SPENDING AN INTERPRETATION OF THE TRANSMISSION MECHANISM

The nature of the relationship between money and effective demand is the subject of a vast body of scholarship in the economics discipline. The present section will offer an interpretation of the causal relationship linking open market operations, that is, the purchase and sale of U.S. government securities by the Federal Reserve Open Market Committee in the secondary market for government debt, and changes in the volume of spending for a particular category of final goods defined as consumer durables. Chapter 2 reviewed the literature which sets forth well known interpretations of the transmission mechanism based on interest rate, net wealth, or portfolio adjustment effects. The contrast between those treatments of the transmission mechanism and the interpretation in the present section can be summarized briefly. The volume of consumer durable spending depends in part on the flow of consumer credit extensions obtained by the household sector which in turn depends partly on the willingness of installment lenders to accommodate the demand for credit regulated to the household finance motive to liquidity. Consumer installment receivables are held in the portfolios of the various consumer lending institutions because they are a source of income in excess of lender's cost. Open market operations impact on the flow of consumer credit extensions, and hence the level of consumer durable spending, by virtue of the effect on such operations on lender's cost and thus the profitability of consumer lending operations. The transmission mechanism described here is based on the assumption that lender's cost is sensitive to movements in the complex of short term interest rates. It will be argued that this is in fact a realistic assumption. Moreover, it is asserted that the sensitivity of lender's cost to short term interest rates has become more pronounced as a result of three developments of recent years: (1) The widespread adoption of sophisticated cash-management techniques on the part of institutional depositors; (2) the proliferation and growing acceptance of money substitutes; and (3) the removal of ceilings on interest paid by depository institutions which were imposed under the Federal Reserve's Regulation Q.

Under the fractional reserve system instituted under the Federal Reserve Act of 1913, commercial banks are legally required to hold a specified sum on account against their deposit liabilities. As the story is typically told in money and banking textbooks, banks are constrained with respect to the volume of loans they can safely make by their reserve position. Hence the power of the Federal Reserve Bank to influence the volume of lending activity, and the stock of money appearing as a result of such activity, essentially derives from its capacity to influence the reserve position of commercial banks. This is accomplished primarily through open market operations. The concept of "reserve-constrained" deposit expansion is consistent with the theoretical notion of an "exogenously" determined nominal money stock that is determined independent of variables such as the level of planned transactions, the level of money wages, the preferences of wealth holding units, with respect to the division of portfolios between money and the less liquid assets. Given a stable, predictable relationship between the quantity of high-powered money and the nominal money stock, the FED may effectively target the growth rate of the money stock by conducting its open money operations in such a way that the quantity of high-powered money in existence is sufficient to achieve the desired growth rate.[15]

But is the volume of lending activity reserve-constrained? That is to say is it realistic to treat money stock as an exogenous variable?

Two points need to be made here. First, it is not within the power of the FED to prevent the nominal money stock from falling below some threshold level. In credit-money economies a large proportion of the nominal money stock takes the form of bank deposits. Transactions deposits came into existence primarily by way of loan. Hence a decrease in the demand for bank credit must necessarily result in a diminution of the nominal money stock. Keynes, as well as Davidson, has argued that one thing which distinguishes money from "all other goods" is that money has a zero, or negligible, elasticity of productivity, meaning that the creation of additional demand deposits in favor of borrowers requires a negligible commitment of real resources.[16] An important implication of this special property of money is that there can never be an excess supply of bank deposits inasmuch as these deposits cannot come into existence unless there is a demand for them.[17] That is to say that the nature of bank-created money is such that banks *do not* manufacture and inventory bank deposits in anticipation of sales to willing borrowers. Hence, owing to a lack of willing borrowers, the stock of bank money may fall precipitously and no amount of activity by the FED in the secondary bond market can reverse such a trend.

A more complicated issue concerns the extent to which the FED, by the conduct of its open market operations, can place an upper limit on the volume of credit expansion throughout the banking system. On one level, the debate often hinges upon whether one regards the FED's support function to be inherently more important than its control function. That is to say that there is fairly wide agreement that the FED could severely constrain the capacity of commercial banks to accommodate credit demand by households and firms. However, the pursuit of such a strategy would require the FED to abdicate its central responsibility, which is to provide for the elasticity of reserves to the banking system in accord with the need of commerce and to stabilize the prices of financial assets which are held by member banks. For instance, Basil Moore has noted that a major source of disagreement between the monetarists and the Post-Keynesians involves contrasting perspectives with respect to the FED's major function:

> Insofar as money itself is concerned perhaps the most fundamental point of difference between post-Keynesians and mainstream economists concern their views as to how the stock of money comes into existence. Post-Keynesians, in sharp contrast to monetarists, regard the stock of money as being simply endogenous, responding and accommodating to changes in the level of money wages. In his *Treatise*, Keynes insisted that money "comes into existence along with debts"--in other words, that the supply of money is related to production contracts and any debts which they necessitate. Money does not enter the system like manna from heaven--or from the sky via Milton Friedman's helicopter. Nor is it simply the creature of the central bank's policies. The central bank determines the stock of legal tender, or what is called the high-powered money base. The public decides the amount of legal tender it wishes to deposit with the banking system and other near-bank financial intermediaries, and the banks decide the amount they wish to maintain as cash reserves and the amount they wish to hold as earnings assets. Conventional analysis assumes that because these ratios are stable, the money stock is exogenous. This point of view ignores completely the historical fact that the purpose of central banks has been to accommodate the stock of money to changes in the needs for trade. Post-Keynesians rank the supportive responsibilities of central banks above their control duties [in ital.].[18]

Moore outlined the implications of an "endogenous" money stock in a recent paper:

> Money endogeneity implies that central banks do not exogenously determine the quantity of credit money in existence, but rather the price at which it is supplied, that is, the short-term interest rate. The money supply is endogenously determined by market forces. Credit money is credit driven, so that loans make deposits rather than the reserve. In all modern economies, so long as borrowers have large unutilized lines of credit or overdraft facilities, the quantity of loans outstanding is determined by bank borrowers,

> not by banks. But the supply of credit money is also demand determined.
>
> The central argument for the endogeneity of credit money may be very simply put: Banks are price setters and quantity takers in both their retail loan and their deposit markets.[19]

Moore has inferred the horizontality of the bank credit flow supply schedule on the basis of data which indicate that unutilized overdraft facilities in the United States are very substantial, perhaps equal to as much as one-third of the reported nominal money stock. Moore's argument seems to run something like this: If IBM has unutilized overdraft facilities, it must be the case that, within a range, the credit supply schedule is horizontal since borrowers have obtained all the credit they wish at prevailing bank-administered interest rates.

As was argued in Chapter 4, section 4.3, installment lenders are to a very important extent quantity-makers as well as price-makers. A credit supply schedule is only relevant provided one has been granted credit. Potential borrowers are not viewed as homogeneous by lenders concerned with the likelihood of their making good on contractual debt obligations. Hence there will always be a set of potential installment borrowers who will not qualify under the standards of credit worthiness set by installment lenders. Thus, some potential borrowers are quantity-rationed in the market for credit. Moreover, quantity-rationing need not depend on "reserve-constrained" deposit expansion. The phenomena of quantity-rationing in the market for consumer loans is therefore generally consistent with Moore's definition of an endogenously determined money stock. The basic difference is that the approach here assigns a much more important role to commercial banks and other installment lenders in determining the volume of credit expansion. The two approaches are in total agreement in that they regard the short-term interest rate, and not the nominal money stock, as the FEDs primary control variable. Figure 6-1 is a schematic diagram which illustrates a step-by-step chain of causation which begins

Figure 6-1
Open Market Operations and Consumer Durable Spending: The Transmission Mechanism

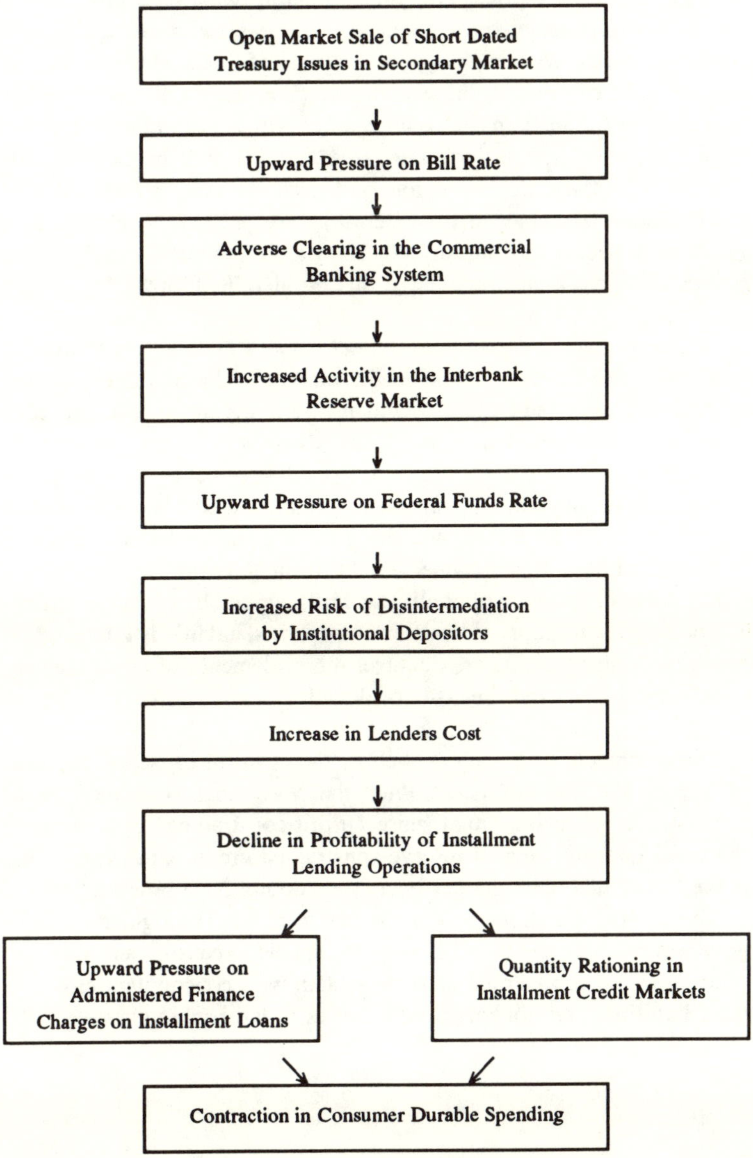

with the open market sale of short-dated Treasury securities in the secondary market by representatives of the FEDs Open Market Committee and ends with a contraction of consumer durable spending.

Assuming that the primary effect of open market activity by the FED is to impinge on the prices and yields of short-dated securities, does it follow that interest charges on newly issued installment credits will fluidly adjust to reflect a change in the price of financial assets such as equities. In contrast to these markets, there exists no set of forces operating in the installment credit market which guarantee that yields on debts issued in the "primary issue" market will be brought into equality with those debts previously issued. Hence, interest rates on newly issued consumer credit extensions are unlikely to change as a result of portfolio substitution effects. Ralph Young, formerly of the Federal Reserve Board, addressed this problem as follows:

> Use of credit by consumers is not subject to direct restriction by higher interest rates in the credit market. Consumer credits are generally extended on fairly standardized terms and at relatively high and inflexible credit charges. Thus, changes in interest rates in the credit market have a less than corresponding effect on the charge for credit to consumers. Nevertheless, the interest cost is one important element in lender's cost, and the general tightness or ease tends to be transmitted to consumer credit through its influence on the strictness or leniency of credit standards applied by consumer credit-granting institutions. Alterations of credit standards is a method by which lenders in this area control other elements of costs, namely collection costs and the costs of default.[20]

The comments of Young as well as the chain of causation depicted in Figure 6-1 are consistent with the view that consumer credit expansion is in an important sense "profit-constrained" in contrast to the usual interpretation of reserve-constrained credit expansion. That is not to say that open market operations do not have powerful effects on the reserve positions of commercial banks. Through the sale of government securities the FED is quite capable of causing an "adverse" clearing in the commercial banking system with concomitant effect on bank liabilities and nonborrowed reserves in the banking system.[21]

However, bank liabilities and total reserves are not variables which fall outside the control of banking institutions. Standard textbook presentations tend to abstract from the growth and evolution of institutional and banking practices which enable banks to adjust their liabilities, and thereby their reserve positions, to accommodate the demands of borrowers. Chief among these innovations in banking is the technique of "liability management." Moore traces the beginnings of modern liability management to the introduction of the negotiable certificate of deposit in 1961.

> Previously bankers passively accepted whatever deposit liabilities the public wanted to hold with them, and allocated these funds among potential borrowers. Liability management has enabled individual banks to target rates of asset growth and then to adjust liabilities to suit their need for funds, rather than accepting their liability structure and tailoring their assets accordingly. Instead of selling short-term marketable assets to meet liquidity needs, banks now rely on their ability to borrow money when needed.[22]

Other banking practices which fall into the category of liability management include the sale of negotiable CDs in the Eurodollar market, borrowing in the interbank (federal funds) market, and the sale of bank-held government securities under repurchase agreement. In each case banks augment their holdings of borrowed reserves. Hence the commercial banking system is capable, within constraints imposed by a legal fractional reserve system with contemporaneous reserve accounting, to maintain a given flow of credit extensions in the face of contractionary monetary policy by substituting borrowed reserves for nonborrowed reserves. However, this cannot occur without impacting upon the price of reserves, which constitutes an important element of lenders cost. For example, an open market sale for securities by the FED should, *ceteris paribus*, cause an increase in borrowing in the federal funds market. This in turn would exert pressure on the price of borrowed reserves, i.e., the federal funds rate.

Another factor works in combination with the elements described in the preceding paragraph to exert pressure on the lending cost as a consequence of contractionary monetary policy. As was stated at the outset of this section, three developments have tended to make lenders' cost more sensitive to movements in the complex of short term interest rates. These developments were defined as: (1) The widespread adoption of sophisticated cash-management techniques on the part of institutional depositors; (2) the proliferation of highly liquid near-monies; and (3) the removal, in March 1980, of Regulation Q interest ceilings on savings and time deposits at depository institutions. The first two developments have had the effect of increasing the elasticity of substitution between bank money and near monies and for the most part blurring the practical distinction between the two. Hence, commercial banks face the risk of "deposit shift" or disintermediation of major institutional depositors out of bank money and into near monies whenever there is an increase in the yields of financial assets. To reduce this risk, banks must offer yields on savings and time deposits which are competitive with those offered by money substitutes. The removal of Regulation Q ceilings make this a viable, if not necessary, option. The effect on bank lending operations of the increase in the elasticity of portfolio substitution can be put simply: It means that a smaller proportion of lenders' cost will be fixed in money terms than would otherwise be the case. Since repayments on the existing stock of consumer receivables are fixed in money terms, the spread between lenders' cost, as proxied by the federal funds, and interest charges on installment debt contracts will narrow anytime there is an increase in lenders' cost. In short, consumer lending operations will become a less profitable proposition from the standpoint of lending institutions.

Installment lenders could react in one of three ways to an increase in lenders' cost which erodes profit margins on consumer loans. First, banks could continue to accommodate all household borrowers who meet the prevailing credit standards at an unchanged bank-administered interest rate, thereby accepting lower profit margins. Or, lending institutions could adjust administered rates to reflect the change in lenders' cost, in which case the decline in household borrowing and durable spending would depend on the interest elasticity of household demand for finance. A third option would entail quantity-rationing. As was argued in Chapter 4, the risk of default on the part of a particular household borrower with a given age, income, credit, and employment profile can be predicted reasonably well through the application of actuarial principles. Thus, financial institutions can roughly predict cost savings in the form of reduced charge-offs and collection costs that would be realized through a tightening of the minimum standards of credit worthiness. As a practical matter, credit rationing takes the form of the crowding out of marginal borrowers under stricter credit standards. For example, where credit scoring systems are used, potential borrowers are rationed when there is an increase in the minimum point score required to qualify for credit. Shay and Dunkelberg studied the effects of credit scoring systems on credit card use in New York and found that a substantial proportion of New York residents holding credit cards during the period would not have qualified under slightly tougher credit standards.[23]

Of course lenders may pursue a strategy which includes both options two and three. The end result will be a contraction in the flow of installment extensions to the household sector and a corresponding decline in spending for consumer durable goods.

6.5 THE EFFECT OF DIRECT AND INDIRECT CREDIT CONTROLS IN THE 1980 AND 1981-1982 RECESSIONS

Apart from the most recent contractionary episode, there is little evidence to support the contention that credit availability effects are a major factor underlying post WWII slumps in durable goods spending. Rather, it appears that the supply of credit schedule facing households has been relatively elastic. Moreover, credit conditions have been such that financial institutions have been able to accommodate the enormous secular increase in the household demand for credit without a tightening of terms. Hence, quarterly fluctuations in the growth rate of installment extensions or changes in the level of household debt outstanding have resulted primarily from changes in the demand for credit.[24] However, the evidence does indicate that discretionary monetary policy, in the form of both direct and indirect credit controls, was effective in attenuating the growth rate of installment extensions as well as debt outstanding beginning in 1978 (see Table 6-4).

Though there exists no device equivalent to the high employment budget to detect periodic shifts in the conduct of monetary policy, the statement that FED policy was "contractionary" in the 1979-1982 period would not generate much controversy.[25] The sustained increase in the general price level experienced throughout the 1970's combined with the rising influence of the New Quantity theorists led to a basic

Table 6-4

Consumer Durable Spending, Growth Rate in Installment Debt Outstanding, and the Debt to Income Ratio, 1977-1982

Year and Quarter		Net Change in Consumption Expenditures for Durables (Annual Rate, Billions of 1982 Dollars)	Annual Growth Rate in Installment Debt Outstanding (percent)	Ratio of Outstanding Installment Debt to Personal Disposable Income
1977:	1	10.0	18.1	14.9
	2	5.1	17.6	15.1
	3	4.4	15.6	15.2
	4	4.9	17.5	15.5
1978:	1	-8.5	16.7	15.8
	2	19.8	20.8	16.0
	3	-1.5	16.0	16.2
	4	3.0	15.8	16.3
1979:	1	-5.0	17.5	16.6
	2	-6.0	13.7	16.8
	3	8.0	13.2	16.9
	4	-7.5	10.4	16.9
1980:	1[a]	-2.8	7.4	16.7
	2	-28.7	-8.3	16.2
	3[*]	10.8	.5	15.7
	4	5.9	2.2	15.2
1981:	1	10.1	6.9	15.0
	2	-10.3	6.9	15.2
	3	7.1	7.8	15.2
	4	-15.3	.4	15.2
1982:	1	7.3	5.0	15.1
	2	1.4	6.5	14.9
	3	2.7	2.8	14.9
	4	10.2	5.0	15.1

[a]Credit controls in effect.

[*]Credit controls discontinued.

Source: *Business Conditions Digest*, series 233 and 227, and the *Federal Reserve Bulletin*, Domestic Financial Statistics, Table 1.57.

Figure 6-2

Consumer Durable Spending, 1979-1983

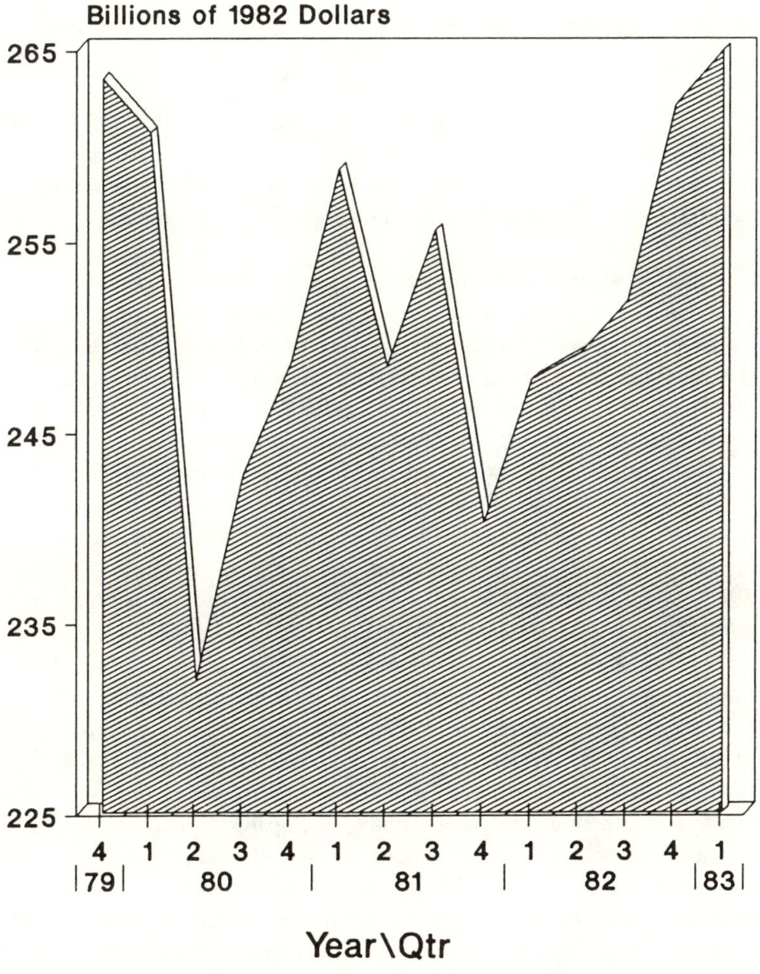

Source: *Business Conditions Digest*, series 233.

the FED's operating procedure in October, 1979. Prior to that time, the FED's discount and open market operations were based on control of the federal funds rate, i.e., the overnight rate for borrowed reserves, as a device for targeting the growth rate of monetary aggregates.[26] Beginning in October, 1979, the FED's strategy involved the day-to-day targeting of unborrowed reserves. Steven Axilrod of the Federal Reserve summarized the practical import of the FED's change in procedure:

> The shift to the new procedure, which meant that day-to-day fluctuations in the funds rate would freely reflect variations in the market demand for reserves, was made in an effort to find a more reliable way to control the money supply in the longer run.[27]

The FED's reluctance to supply reserves to the banking system resulted in a marked increase in volume in the federal funds market with consequent upward pressure on the cost of borrowed reserves. The federal funds rate, which stood at 4.6% in March 1977, rose steadily thereafter to a peak of nearly 18% in the 2nd quarter of 1981. The indirect credit controls in combination with the consumer credit restraint program put into effect in March 1980 greatly curtailed the extent of commercial bank participation in the consumer finance industry (see Table 6-5). Extensions of installment credit by commercial banks fell a staggering $18.6 billion between 1978 and 1981. In addition, whereas commercial banks accounted for approximately 54% of total installment extensions in the 2nd quarter of 1978, that share fell to 35% immediately after direct controls were imposed in 1980. Of course, it is possible that the decline in extensions by commercial banks was caused primarily by a reduction in the demand for durable goods by households in a situation of falling personal income and rising unemployment. However, if this were true one would expect extensions by finance companies, credit unions, and retailers to decline on a percentage basis in rough proportion to the decline in extensions made by commercial banks. That is, there is no reason to expect that a general reduction in the demand for credit would be expressed in a disproportionate decrease in the demand for

Table 6-5
Consumer Installment Credit Extensions and Repayments to Outstanding Debt, 1977-1982

Quarter	Extensions of Installment Credit by All Suppliers (Millions of 1982 Dollars)	Extensions of Installment Credit by Commercial Banks (Millions of 1982 Dollars)	Change in Commercial Bank Share (percent)	Ratio of Repayments to Outstanding Debt[1]
1977: 1	79,739	37,067	-1.8	.23
2	83,852	41,082	2.5	.23
3	84,194	41,375	.2	.23
4	86,466	43,187	.8	.23
1978: 1	87,783	43,116	-.8	.22
2	93,761	50,283	4.5	.26
3	104,563	50,158	-5.6	.26
4	105,491	49,989	-.6	.25
1979: 1	103,080	48,614	-.5	.25
2	106,767	49,857	-.5	.25
3	104,273	48,370	-.3	.25
4	98,556	44,230	-.5	.24
1980: 1	97,216	42,860	-.9	.24
2[2]	91,297	31,589	-9.4	.24
3	89,291	38,007	8.0	.25
4	90,354	39,211	.8	.25
1981: 1	93,743	38,030	-2.8	.26
2	92,707	39,358	1.9	.25
3	91,757	38,465	-.6	.24
4	84,097	37,534	2.7	.24
1982: 1	82,994	37,398	.5	.24
2	88,111	39,250	-.6	.25
3	82,967	37,435	.6	.24
4	88,627	41,229	1.4	.25

[1]Repayments include liquidations and charge offs.

[2]Credit controls in effect.

Source: *Federal Reserve Bulletin*, Domestic Financial Statistics, Table 1.57 and 1.58.

bank credit. Hence, the decrease in the share of total extensions made by commercial banks was not a purely demand side phenomena. Whereas extensions made by commercial banks fell 37% between 1978 and 1980, total extensions fell by only 2.6% in the same period. Thus while commercial banks were cutting back on their holdings consumer paper, retailers and finance companies were increasing both their volume of extensions and their shares of total installment paper held. For example, extensions made by finance companies increased by more than 4 billion between 1979 and 1981.

Figure 6-3

Net Change in Installment Credit Outstanding, 1979-1983

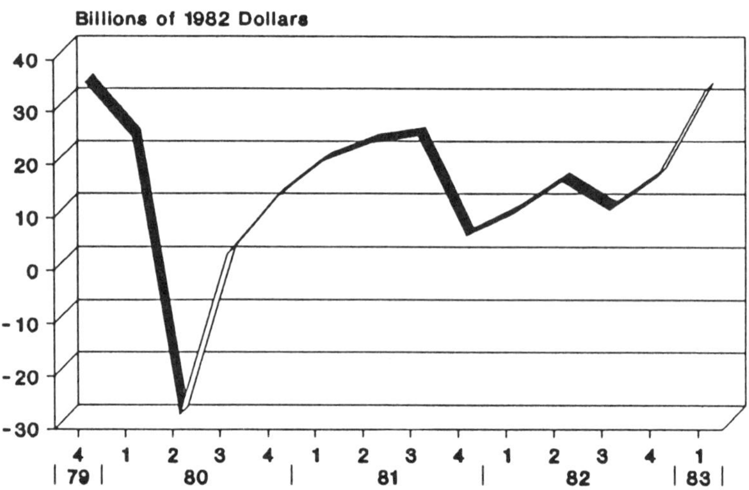

Source: *Business Conditions Digest*, series 113 and 310.

Figure 6-4

Average Percentage Rate, 48 Mo. Car Loan, and the Fed Funds Rate, 1975-1984

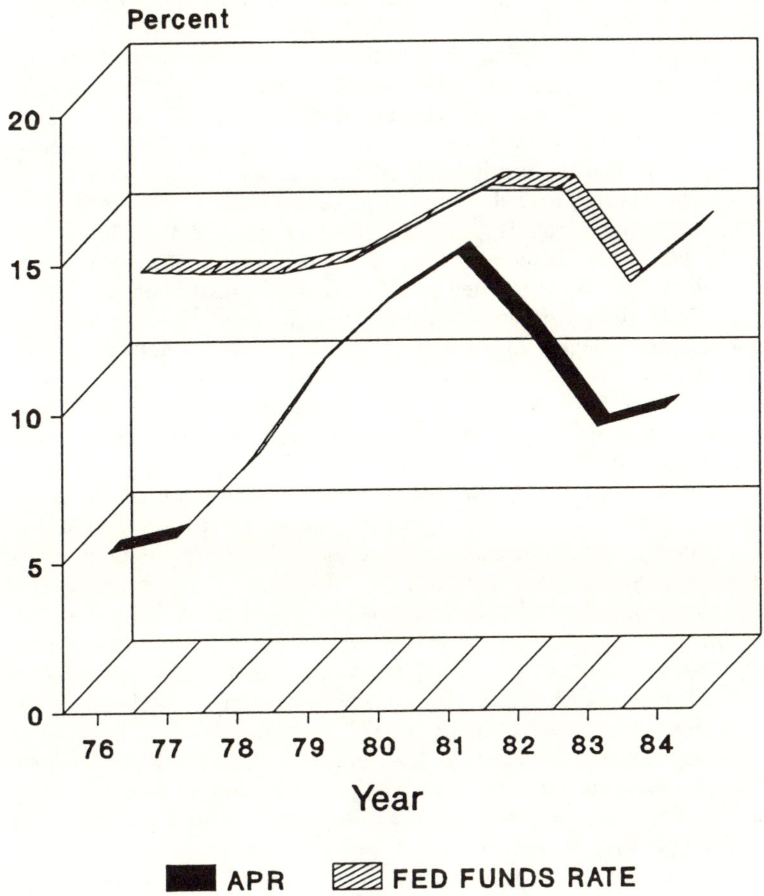

Source: *Federal Reserve Bulletin*, Table 1.56 and *Business Conditions Digest*, series 119.

What factors account for the precipitous decline in commercial bank participation in the consumer finance industry? First, the increase in the cost of borrowed reserves severely eroded profit margins on consumer loans as state usury ceilings prevented finance charges from rising as much as free market rates. The prime rate, which historically tends to be several percentage points below the rate on new auto loans, reached 21% in 1980 whereas the *Federal Reserve Bulletin* survey of terms of consumer lending showed that the most common rate on auto loans was 15%. Figure 6-4 shows the federal funds rate and the average percentage rate (APR) charged by commercial banks on new car loans between 1976 and 1984. It was stated in Chapter 4, section 4.2, that the profitability of installment lending is determined by the spread between the average percentage rate and lenders' cost. The federal funds rate is given as a proxy of lender's cost. Inspection of Table 6-6 reveals the following: (1) The change in Federal Reserve operating procedures resulted in strong upward pressure on the federal funds rate with corresponding effect on lenders' cost; and (2) the average percentage rate charged on new car loans did not fully adjust to reflect the increase in lender's cost. One may infer on the basis of this data that profit margins on installment loans were squeezed due to the reduction in the spread between lender's cost and the average percentage rate.

Another important factor was that many banks reported increased charge offs and collection costs beginning in 1979, though the delinquency rate on installment debt showed a marginal increase in 1979 and 1980 and decreased in 1981. Based on the Federal Reserve's functional cost analysis, Connor and Fergus reported that pretax net earnings of commercial banks on holdings of installment paper, expressed as a percent of credit outstanding, fell below 2 percent in 1980.This figure compares with average net earnings of 2.4 percent on consumer installment credit from 1972 through 1985.[28]

In addition to the indirect controls and subsequent impact on lender's cost, it appears that the credit restraint program made consumer lending a less attractive proposition from the viewpoint of bankers. The Federal Reserve Board conducts a quarterly Survey of Bank Lending Practices. On May 15, 1980, two months after direct controls were imposed, 76 of 120 senior loan officers surveyed, or 63%, reported that they were either "moderately less willing" or "much less willing" to make consumer installment loans as compared to their position of February 15, 1980. Only 7 of 120, or about 6 percent, of bankers surveyed indicated they were "more willing" to make consumer loans. This attitude was reflected in an 11.3 billion decrease in commercial bank extensions in the 2nd quarter of 1980.

Though FED policy was extremely effective in constraining consumer credit extension by the commercial banking system in the between January and June of 1980, it was not nearly so effective in regulating the flow of extensions by all suppliers of consumer credit. Consumers who could not qualify for credit under tougher standards set forth by banks were often able to substitute credit extended by finance companies, retailers, and credit unions. A basic question arises: In so far as all suppliers of consumer credit are subject to usury ceilings and must finance their holdings of consumer paper with borrowed funds, why is it that finance companies and retailers were more willing to accommodate household credit demand than commercial banks in the last cyclical downturn? There are two plausible explanations. First, several of the large finance companies such as General Motors Acceptance Corporation are subsidiaries of a major durable goods manufacturer. Under conditions of tightness in financial markets they act as lenders of last resort to provide the liquidity necessary for the purchase of their parent companies output. In the case of retail establishments which supply "point-of-sale" credit, increasing costs can be passed on to the consumer in the form of higher retail prices.[29] Thus the FED was frustrated in its attempt to target the growth of monetary aggregates by the fact that nonbank suppliers of consumer credit have motives other than profit maximization with respect to their holdings of consumer receivables.

This section has assessed the impact of Federal Reserve policy on consumer spending in the 1980 and 1981-1982 recessions. The effects of the contractionary monetary regime adopted by the FED in 1979 represent a good fit with the interpretation of the transmission mechanism described in section 6.4 of this chapter. The conduct of open market operations during the period led to a sharp increase in the complex of short-term interest rates. This development in turn resulted in upward pressure on the federal funds rate, a key element in lenders' cost. Commercial banks sharply curtailed their participation in the market for installment credit in response to a decline in the profitability of those operations. In summary, it has been argued that the direct and indirect credit controls imposed between 1979 and 1982 were successful in limiting the flow of consumer credit extensions supplied by the commercial banking system but were only moderately effective in regulating the flow of credits granted by all suppliers of consumer finance. Credit rationing by banks was offset to some degree by an increase in the volume of extensions granted by finance companies and retail establishments. Nevertheless, contractionary monetary policy remains an important factor in explaining the consumer durable goods slump in the most recent contractionary phase of the business cycle.

6.6 SUMMARY

This chapter has evaluated the impact of various policy initiatives of the Federal Reserve System on the volume of consumer durable goods spending. The basic unifying principle of this book is restated as follows: Because the purchase of big-ticket consumer durable goods ordinarily creates a cash flow problem for household spending units, the volume of consumer durable spending depends partly on the willingness of households to incur installment debt liabilities and partly on the fluid operation of consumer credit markets in supplying a steady flow of installment credit extensions to the household sector. Chapter 6 has been primarily concerned with tracing out the specific channels through which the various policy initiatives of the FED affect supply-side conditions in markets for consumer installment credit.

Section 6.1 discussed the Federal Reserve's Regulation A, which pertains to the eligibility of different categories of bank assets for discount at the FED's discount window. It was stated that a liberal stance toward the eligibility of consumer installment receivables for discount would, other things being equal, contribute to bankers' willingness to hold such assets by rendering installment receivables more liquid. The Credit Control Act of 1969 was the subject of section 6.2. Particular emphasis was given to the controls imposed during the Carter Administration in 1980. Section 6.3 evaluated the effect of direct regulation of hire-purchase terms on installment contracts in attenuating the volume of household borrowing and durable spending. Section 6.4 presented an interpretation of the monetary transmission mechanism linking the conduct of Federal Reserve open market operations to changes in the volume of consumer durable spending. The key element of the transmission mechanism was given as the effect of open market operations on lender's cost, the profitability of consumer lending operations, and hence the willingness of commercial banks to accommodate the household demand for finance. Building on the arguments set forth in the previous sections of Chapter 6, section 6.5 analyzed the effectiveness of both direct and indirect policy initiatives of the FED in restraining the volume of installment credit expansion during the 1979-1982 recession. It was argued that the contractionary regime adopted by the FED beginning in 1978 resulted in a sharp curtailment of commercial bank consumer credit extensions and was partly responsible for the dramatic slump in consumer durable goods sales between 1979 and 1982.

NOTES

1. The desire for earnings assets which offer a high degree of liquidity might offer a partial explanation of the recent pressure brought to bear by the banking community for the repeal of the Glass-Steagall Act of 1933, which prohibits depository institutions from engaging in securities underwriting activities. The repeal of this legislation might conceivably reinforce the recent trend toward the "securitization" of assets such as mortgage notes and debts collateralized by automobiles. Commercial banks would underwrite issues of consumer durable securities and act as market-makers in the secondary market for such assets, thereby maintaining their liquidity.

2. Knodell (1987), p. 693.

3. These guidelines are contained in the Federal Reserve's Regulation A.

4. See Regulation A, subsection D, "Kinds of Collateral Which May Be Used As Security Against Such Advances," published in *Regulations of the Board of Governors of the Federal Reserve.*

5. These figures are based on estimates made by the Federal Reserve Board in 1953. See Smith, *ibid.*, p. 354.

6. See, for example, Peter Temin (1976).

7. Epstein and Ferguson (1984), p. 969. For a detailed look at changes in the composition of bank portfolios in the Depression, see Epstein and Ferguson, *ibid.*, Tables I and II, pp. 970-971.

8. Installment contracts offered at the point-of-sale and then discounted appear as "paper purchased" indirectly in the consumer credit statistics, Table 1.56, *Federal Reserve Bulletin.*

9. Borrowing on credit card accounts is typically weakest in the first quarter of any given year. The consumer credit statistics are not seasonally adjusted.

10. Teters (1979), p. 467.

11. See, for example, Enthoven (1957).

12. See Hamburger and Zwick, *op. cit.*

13. Cmnd. 827 (HMSO, August 1959).

14. *Ibid.*, para. 469.

15. High-powered money consists of currency and coin in circulation and reserves on account of commercial banks.

16. Davidson, *op. cit.*, p. 215.

17. Davidson argues that the "spot price" of money cannot fall below

the "long run supply price" in a world of uncertainty. That is, there can never be a cantango in the spot market for money." See Davidson, *ibid.*, pp. 215-217.

18. Moore (1979), pp. 125-126.

19. Moore (1988), p. 381.

20. Young (1953), pp. 225-226.

21. A bank is said to suffer an adverse clearing when, after the check clearing process is complete, its claims against other banks fall short of the claims other banks have against it. Walter C. Neale defines a central bank as "a bank so large, with so many financial assets to sell, and with so much capacity to create acceptable means of payment, that by itself it can force almost all other banks into adverse clearings with itself, or by itself assure almost all other banks of favourable clearings." See Neale (1976), p. 75.

22. Moore (1986), p. 449.

23. See Shay and Dunkelberg (1975).

24. Peterson is a notable dissenter on this point. Peterson found that commercial banks cut back disproportionately on installment extensions in the "tight money" phases of 1969-1 to 1970-2 and 1973-1 to 1974-4. See Peterson (1976).

25. A statement typical of this period by Paul Volcker, speaking before the House Committee on Banking, Finance, and Urban Affairs on November 19, 1980: "Looking at the recent situation, I believe it should be unambiguously clear that the Federal Reserve has been leaning hard against excessive monetary growth and that we mean to maintain firm control as we look ahead." See Volcker (1981), p. 13.

26. The FED formally announced its intention of targeting monetary aggregates, specifically M_1, M_2, and M_3, in 1978.

27. Axilrod (1982), p. 19.

28. See Connor and Fergus (1987), p. 2

29. Lynch (1968) found that retail prices of durable goods were significantly higher in Arkansas than in states with less restrictive usury ceilings.

Chapter 7

Conclusions And Policy Implications

The purpose of this study has been to describe and analyze the specific channels through which monetary factors are transmitted to the behavior of consumer durable spending. In contrast to theoretical and empirical treatments of the monetary transmission mechanism which are based on interest rate effects, net wealth effects, or portfolio adjustment effects, the interpretation of the transmission mechanism presented in this analysis places emphasis on the relationship between the phenomena of bank money-creation and the level of consumer durable spending.

It was argued that the development of wide and deep markets for consumer durable goods in the United States necessarily required the corresponding development of markets for consumer installment credit. The purchase of a big ticket durable item ordinarily creates a cash flow problem for the household and as such a large proportion of consumer durable purchases are debt-financed. The volume of consumer durable spending thus depends partly on the willingness of households to incur contractually enforceable debt obligations. Moreover, the volume of durable spending is strongly influenced by the willingness of installment lenders to accommodate the household demand for finance. The activity of bank money-creation, in which commercial banks create checkable deposits in favor of household borrowers, is viewed as crucial to sustaining the aggregate demand for consumer durable goods.

The volume of consumer durable spending depends upon the existence of mechanisms which provide a regularized flow of consumer credit extensions to the household sector. Hence any factor or combination of factors which obstruct the channels of consumer finance are also likely to exert a depressing effect on durable spending.

Through the application of partial equilibrium analysis, the thesis delineated the various sources of instability in markets for consumer installment credit. These potential sources of instability were put under two general headings. The first was defined as "the changing attitude of the household toward debt obligations." It was argued in Chapter 3 that episodic shifts in attitudes toward debt are capable of generating a surge in consumer durable spending. Conversely, a groundswell of opinion unfavorable to the practice of installment buying may precipitate an episode of what was termed "household debt deflation." Debt deflation is most likely to occur after a sustained period of strong household borrowing, when existing contractual debt obligations exert considerable pressure on the household budget constraint.

A second source of instability was defined as "changing supply-side conditions in installment credit markets." Chapter 4 examined the factors which condition the ability and/or willingness of installment lenders to hold installment receivables in their portfolios of earning assets. The primary determinant of the willingness of commercial banks to create deposits in favor of installment borrowers was defined as the profitability of consumer lending operations. The study described the factors which determine the relative profitability of consumer lending. Chapter 5 analyzed the causal relationship between consumer credit expansion and inflation.

Chapter 6 evaluated the effects of Federal Reserve policy on conditions in consumer credit markets. Aside from the use of hire-purchase controls or direct restrictions on the composition of bank portfolios, it was stated that policy initiatives of the Federal Reserve System are connected to the volume of installment borrowing by virtue of their effect on the profitability of installment lending. Evidence was given in support of the thesis that the contractionary regime adopted by the Federal Reserve in 1979 in combination with the direct credit controls imposed in 1980 severely eroded profit margins on installment debt contracts. These developments in turn precipitated a sharp curtailment in consumer credit extensions made by commercial banks beginning in the fourth quarter of 1979. It was argued that Federal Reserve policy was a contributing factor to the durable goods slump experienced in the U.S. during the 1980 and 1981-1982 recessions.

An important issue concerns the appropriate set of public policies regarding the practice of installment buying in general and the consumer credit industry in particular. That the practice of installment buying has contributed to problems of financial distress on the part of many households is beyond dispute. However, a key point which emerges from the thesis is that there is a basic disparity between the flow of output which society is capable of producing with its given endowments of economic resources, technical and organizational knowledge, and the ability of society to purchase that output on the basis of current income flows. In an important sense, the development of markets for consumer credit and the liberalization of attitudes toward installment buying can be viewed as a social, institutional, and economic adjustment to a cash flow problem of enormous magnitude. It is difficult if not impossible to conceive of an alternative solution to this problem within the context of contemporary economic, social, and political organization.

What can be said about the appropriate set of macroeconomic policies, and particularly monetary policies, with regard to the functioning of markets for consumer finance? The basic function of the Federal Reserve System is to provide for elasticity of reserves to the commercial banking system in accommodation of the legitimate credit requirements of firms and households. Surely the household demand for finance ought to be regarded as a "legitimate" credit requirement if for no other reason than a high volume of household borrowing is a necessary condition for the existence of a thriving consumer durable goods sector in market-oriented economies. However, the Federal Reserve Bank seems to have evolved into an anti-inflation agency during the past two decades. This development is the result of the resurgence of the quantity theory of money as a dominant economic doctrine as well as a political and ideological stalemate with respect to alternative inflation policies. The use of open market operations in a heretofore fruitless attempt by the Federal Reserve to target monetary aggregates produces powerful side effects and conflicts with the FED's basic function. Chapter 6 described the effects of the contractionary regime adopted by the FED in 1979 on consumer durable spending. It should also be noted that the day-to-day targeting of borrowed reserves had powerful repercussions with respect to the entire complex of interest rates and devastated interest-sensitive sectors of the economy such as residential construction. The lesson of the 1979-1982 period seems to be that one can indeed diffuse inflationary pressure through the use of contractionary monetary policy; however, this can be accomplished only at the expense of billions of dollars of lost output and high unemployment. Moreover, such policies threaten stability in the banking system. A strong case can be made that alternative inflation policies involve less pain and more fairness. An example would be Tax Based Incomes Policies as suggested by Sidney Weintraub, among others.[1]

That is not to say that some types of credit controls might not be purposefully used. For example, the direct control of hire-purchase terms might be appropriate under certain circumstances, such as in the case of shortages or bottlenecks due to strike activity. Also, it may be desirable to use direct controls to smooth the growth rate of installment debt outstanding. The previous two cyclical contractions in the U.S. were preceded by a rapid build-up of household indebtedness. Other things being equal, an increase in the growth rate of per capita indebtedness above its historical mean requires that an increasing fraction of disposable income in succeeding months or quarters be claimed by debt servicing. Hence, policies designed to prevent a sudden build-up of debt could ease short term pressure exerted on the budget constraint by debt servicing. Such a policy would also likely reduce the possibility of an episode of household debt deflation.

The general subject of consumer durable spending and its relationship to installment borrowing is one that offers several possibilities for future research. A possible topic of analysis would be to examine the likely consequences of consumer debt "securitization" on the price and availability of consumer finance. Secondary markets for installment receivables continue to be poorly developed as compared to those for financial assets. However, the banking industry continues to lobby for the repeal of the Glass-Steagall Act which would allow commercial banks to enter the securities underwriting business. If highly developed secondary markets for installment debt were to evolve as a consequence of a change in the basic role of commercial banks in the installment credit industry, it seems likely that there would be a fundamental change in the way in which the price of installment debt gets determined. Administered pricing models such as the one suggested in Chapter 4 are not adequate to the analysis of pricing in organized spot markets.

An issue of broader importance concerns the impact of bank regulatory reform and modern cash-management techniques on the cost commercial banks must bear to attract short and medium term deposits. We now live in an economy in which even comparatively modest business enterprises seek the most profitable outlet for their liquid assets. From a purely economic perspective, the widespread adoption of sophisticated cash management techniques surely ranks as one of the most important institutional changes of the 1980s. With the proliferation of money substitutes, the competition for deposits by financial intermediaries has been greatly intensified. This increased competition has created something like a ratchet effect on lenders' cost. The secular increase in lenders' cost, as revealed by the secular behavior of the interbank reserve rate and rates on short and medium term commercial deposits, may in turn have serious repercussions with regard to the price of business credit, mortgage money, and consumer installment credit.

NOTE

1. See Weintraub (1978), Chapter 6.

Bibliography

BOOKS

Bain, Joe. *Industrial Organization*, 2nd ed. New York: Wiley and Sons, 1968.

Brittain, John A. *Inheritance and the Inequality of Material Wealth*. Washington: The Brookings Institution, 1978.

Davidson, Paul. *Money and the Real World*, 2nd ed. London: The Macmillan Press, 1978.

Duesenberry, James S. *Income, Saving, and the Theory of Consumer Behavior*. Cambridge: Harvard University Press, 1949.

Eichner, Alfred S. *The Megacorp and Oligopoly*. New York: M. E. Sharpe, 1982.

Fisher, Irving. *The Rate of Interest*. New York: Macmillan, 1911.

Friedman, Milton. *A Theory of the Consumption Function*. Princeton: Princeton University Press, 1957.

_______ and Anna J. Schwartz. *Monetary Trends in the U.S. and the U.K.*. Chicago: University of Chicago Press, 1982.

Goldsmith, Raymond W. *The National Wealth of the United States in the Postwar Period*. Princeton: Princeton University Press, 1962.

Gurley, John G., and Edward S. Shaw. *Money in a Theory of Finance*. Washington: The Brookings Institution, 1959.

Harris, Laurence. *Monetary Theory*. New York: McGraw Hill, 1981.

Hicks, John. *The Crisis in Keynesian Economics*. New York: Basic Books, 1974.

Hume, David. *Essays*. London: Longmans, Green, and Company, 1912.

Hendricks, Gary, Kenwood C. Youmans, and Janet Keller. *Consumer Durables and Installment Debt: A Study of American Households*. Ann Arbor: Institute for Social Research, 1973.

Johnson, Robert W. *Methods of Standing Consumer Finance Charges*. New York: Graduate School of Business, Columbia University, 1961.

Kalecki, Michael. *Essays in the Theory of Economic Fluctuations*. London: George Allen and Unwin, 1939.

Kendrick, John W. *The Formation and Stocks of Total Capital*. New York: Columbia University Press, 1976.

Keynes, John Maynard. *The General Theory of Employment, Interest, and Money*. New York: Harcourt Brace, 1936.

________. *Treatise on Money*. London: Macmillan, 1930.

Lampman, Robert J. *The Share of Top Wealth-Holders in National Wealth, 1922-1956*. Princeton: Princeton University Press, 1962.

Malkiel, Burton G. *The Term Structure of Interest Rates: Expectations and Behavior Patterns*. Princeton: Princeton University Press, 1966.

Mandell, Lewis. *The Credit Card Industry*. Boston: Twayne Publishers, 1990.

Marshall, Alfred. *Principles of Economics*, 8th ed. New York: Macmillan, 1930.

Mars, Wallace P. *Consumer Credit Finance Charges*. New York: Columbia University Press, 1965.

Minsky, Hyman P. *John Maynard Keynes*. New York: Columbia University Press, 1975.

Neale, Walter C. *Monies in Societies*. San Francisco: Chandler and Sharp, 1976.

Patinkin, Don. *Money, Interest, and Prices*, 2nd ed. New York: Harper and Row, 1965.

Pesek, Boris P., and Thomas Saving. *Money, Wealth, and Economic Theory*. New York: Macmillan, 1967.

Porter, Michael E. *Competitive Strategy*. New York: The Free Press, 1980.

Robertson, Dennis H. *Essays in Monetary Theory*. London: Staples Press, 1940.

Robinson, Joan. *What Are the Questions?* New York: M. E. Sharpe, 1980.

________. *The Generalization of the General Theory*, 2nd ed. New York: St. Martin's Press, 1979.

Temin, Peter. *Did Monetary Forces Cause the Great Depression?* New York: W. W. Norton, 1976.

Scherer, F. M., A. Beckenstein, E. Kaufer, and R. D. Murphy. *The Economics of Multiplant Operation*. Cambridge: Harvard University Press, 1975.

Schumpeter, Joseph A. *The Theory of Economic Development*. Cambridge: Harvard University Press, 1954.

________. *Capitalism, Socialism, and Democracy*. New York: Harper and Row, 1942.

Shackle, G. L. S. *The Years of High Theory*. Cambridge: Cambridge University Press, 1967.

. *Uncertainty in Economics*. Cambridge: Cambridge University Press, 1955.

Veblen, Thorstein. *The Theory of the Leisure Class*. New York: Mentor Books, 1953.

Von Mises, Ludwig. *The Theory of Money and Credit*. New Haven: Yale University Press, 1953.

Weintraub, Sidney. *Capitalism's Inflation and Unemployment Crisis*. Reading: Addison-Wesley Publishing, 1978.

ARTICLES

Adams, Walter, and W. Brock. "The Automobile Industry," in *The Structure of American Industry*, 7th ed., W. Adams, ed. New York: Macmillan, 1986, 126-171.

Allard, R. J.. "Credit Restrictions and Lag Distributions onConsumer Durable Equations," *Applied Economics*, 11(2), 1979, 77-97.

Axilrod, Stephen. "Monetary Policy, the Money Supply, and the Federal Reserve's Operating Procedure," *Federal Reserve Bulletin*, 68(12), 1982, 13-23.

Ball, R. J., and Pamela S. Drake. "The Impact of Credit Control on Consumer Durable Spending in the U.K., 1957-1961," *Review of Economic Studies*, 30(3), 1963, 181-194.

Barro, Robert. "Are Government Bonds Net Wealth?" *Journal of Political Economy*, 82, November-December 1974, 1095-1117.

_______ and Mark Rush. "Unanticipated Money and Economic Activity," in *Rational Expectations and Economic Policy*, Stanley Fisher, ed. Chicago: University of Chicago Press, 1980, 23-73.

Bean, C. "The Determination of Consumers' Expenditure in the U.K.," Treasury Working Paper No. 4, July 1978.

Bennett, Robert A. "Putting the Homestead Deeper into Hock," Sunday Business Section, *New York Times*, November 24, 1985, 1.

Blinder, Alan S. "Keynes, Lucas, and Scientific Progress," *American Economic Review*, 77(2), May 1987, 130-136.

Bosworth, Barry. "The Stock Market and the Economy," *Brookings Papers on Economic Activity*, 2, 1975, 261-282.

Brechling, F. R. "Monetary Policy and Neoclassical Investment Analysis," in *Issues in Monetary Economics*, H. G. Johnson and A. R. Norbay, eds. (London: Oxford University Press), 1974.

Burch, S. W. "The Aging U.S. Auto Stock: Implications for Demand," *Business Economics*, 18(3), May 1983, 22-26.

Burke, Jim. "Antitrust Laws, Justice Department Guidelines, and the Limits of Concentration," Staff Study, Federal Reserve Board, 1983.

Canner, Glen B., R. Avery, and G. Elliehausen. "Survey of Consumer Finances, 1983," *Federal Reserve Bulletin*, 70(9), September 1984, 679-692.

Canner, Glen B., and Anthony W. Cyrnak. "Determinants of Credit Card Usage Patterns," *Journal of Retail Banking*, 8, Spring/Summer 1986, 9-18.

Canner, Glenn B., and James T. Fergus. "The Economic Effects of Proposed Ceilings on Credit Card Interest Rates," *Federal Reserve Bulletin*, 73(1), January 1987, 1-13.

Clower, Robert W. "A Reconsideration of the Microfoundations of Monetary Theory," *Western Economic Journal*, 6, December 1967, 1-8.

________. "The Keynesian Counterrevolution: A Theoretical Appraisal," in *The Theory of Interest Rates*, F. Hahn and F. Brechling, eds. London: Macmillan, 1965.

Cuthbertson, Keith. "The Determination of Expenditure on Consumer Durables," *National Institute Economic Review*, 3, 1982, 62-72.

De Leeuw, Frank. "Why Capacity Utilization Estimates Differ," *Survey of Current Business*, May 1979, 45-55.

Dessart, W. C. A. M., and A. A. A. Kuylen. "The Nature, Extent, Causes, and Consequences of Problematic Debt Situations," *Journal of Consumer Policy*, 9, September 1986, 311-334.

Enthoven, Alain. "The Growth of Installment Credit and the Future of Prosperity," *American Economic Review*, 47(4), December 1957, 913-929.

Epstein, G., and Thomas Ferguson. "Monetary Policy, Loan Liquidation, and Industrial Conflict," *Journal of Economic History*, 18(2), June 1984, 439-448.

Evans, G. R. "The Evolution of Financial Institutions and the Ineffectiveness of Modern Monetary Policy," *Journal of Economic Issues*, 18(2), June 1984, 439-448.

Evans, Michael K., and Avram Kisselgoff, "The Demand for Consumer Installment Debt and Its Effect on Consumption," in *The Brookings Model: Some Further Results*. Chicago: University of Chicago Press, 1968.

Fair, R. C. "Consumer Sentiment, The Stock Market, and Consumption Functions," Econometric Research Program Memorandum No. 119, Princeton University, 1971.

Feldstein, Martin. "The Effects of Fiscal Policy When Incomes Are Uncertain: A Contradiction to Ricardian Equivalence," *American Economic Review*, 78(1), March 1988, 14-23.

Forestal, Robert P. "High Debt Levels Hike Risk of Lower Standard of Living," *Fedlines*, Federal Reserve Bank of Atlanta, February 1, 1987, 1-2.

Friedman, Milton. "The Role of Monetary Policy," *American Economic Review*, 58(2), March 1968, 1-17.

________. "The Quantity Theory of Money--A Restatement," in *Studies in the Quantity Theory of Money*, M. Friedman, ed. Chicago: University of Chicago Press, 1956, 3-21.

________ and David Meiselman. "The Relative Stability of Monetary Velocity and the Investment Multiplier in the U.S., 1898-1958," in *Commission on Money and Credit: Stabilization Policies*. Englewood Cliffs: Prentice Hall, 1963, 7-44.

Gilbert, R. A. "Banking Market Structure and Competition: A Survey," *Journal of Money, Credit, and Banking*, 16(2), November 1984, 617-644.

Gordon, R. J. "Why U.S. Wage and Employment Behavior Differs from that in the U.K. and Japan," *Economic Journal*, 92(1), March 1982, 13-44.

________ and J. A. Wilcox. "Monetarist Interpretations of the Great Depression: An Evaluation and Critique," in *Contemporary Views of the Great Depression*, K. Brunner, ed. Hingham: Martinus Nijhoff, 1981, 49-107.

Greenfield, R. L., and Yeager, L. B. "Money and Credit Confused: An Appraisal of Economic Doctrine and Federal Reserve Procedure," *Southern Economic Journal*, 53(2), October 1986, 364-373.

Greer, Douglas F. "Rate Ceilings and Loan Turndowns," *Journal of Finance*, 30(4), December 1975, 1376-1383.

Grieves, R. "The Demand for Consumer Durables," *Journal of Money, Credit, and Banking*, 15(3), August 1983, 316-326.

Hall, Robert E. "Stochastic Implications of the Life Cycle Hypothesis," *Journal of Political Economy*, 86(4), December 1978, 971-987.

Hamburger, M. J. "Interest Rates and the Demand for Consumer Durable Goods," *American Economic Review*, 57(4), December 1967, 1113- 1153.

________ and Burton Zwick. "Installment Credit Controls, Consumer Expenditures, and the Allocation of Real Resources," *Journal of Finance*, 32(4), December 1977, 1557-1569.

Heggestad, A., and William G. Shepard. "The Banking Industry," in *The Structure of American Industry*, 7th ed., W. Adams, ed. New York: Macmillan, 1986, 290-324.

Hymans, S. H. "Consumer Durable Spending: Explanation and Prediction," *Brookings Papers on Economic Activity*, 21(2), March 1970, 441-466.

Jorgenson, Dale W. "Econometric Studies of Investment Behavior," *Journal of Economic Literature*, 9(4), December 1971, 1111-1147.

________ and J. A. Stevenson. "Investment Behavior in U.S. Manufacturing," *Econometrica*, 24(1), April 1967, 169-220.

Juster, Thomas F., and Robert P. Shay, "Consumer Sensitivity to Finance Rates: An Empirical and Analytical Investigation," Occasional Paper No. 88. New York: National Bureau of Economic Research, 1964.

Kader, A. A. "The Stock Market as a Leading Indicator of Economic Activity," *Atlantic Economic Journal*, 13(1), March 1985, 223-227.

Kahn, Alfred E. "Pricing Objectives of Large Companies," *American Economic Review*, 49(3), September 1959, 670-678.

Kalecki, Michael. "The Supply Curve of an Industry Under Imperfect Competition," *Review of Economic Studies*, 7(2), June 1940, 521-532.

Keynes, John Maynard. "The Ex Ante Theory of the Rate of Interest," in *The Collected Writings of John Maynard Keynes*, Volume 14. London: Macmillan, 1973.

Knodell, Jane. "Open Market Operations: Their Evolution and Significance," *Journal of Economic Issues*, 21(2), June 1987, 691-699.

Kowalewski, K. J. "Is the Consumer Overextended," *Economic Commentary*, Federal Reserve Bank of Cleveland, November 15, 1986.

Laumas, G. S., and Ram, R. "The Role of Wealth in Consumption: An Empirical Investigation," *Review of Economic Statistics*, 64(2), May 1982, 204-210.

Lucas, Robert E. "Econometric Policy Evaluation: A Critique," in *Studies in Business Cycle Theory* by R. E. Lucas. Cambridge: MIT Press, 1983, 19-46.

________. "Understanding Business Cycles," in *Studies in Business Cycle Theory* by R. E. Lucas. Cambridge: MIT Press, 1983, 215-239.

Luckett, C. A., and J. D. August. "The Growth of Consumer Debt," *Federal Reserve Bulletin*, 71(6), 389-402.

Lynch, Gordon. "Consumer Credit at 10% Simple: The Arkansas Case," *Law Forum*, Winter 1968, 592-618.

Mankiw, N. G. "Consumer Durables and the Real Interest Rate," *Review of Economic Statistics*, 67(3), August 1985, 353-362.

Maris, B. A. "Indirect Evidence on the Efficacy of Selective Credit Controls: The Case of Consumer Credit," *Journal of Money, Credit, and Banking*, 13(3), August 1981, 388-390.

Markham, J. W. "The Nature and Significance of Price Leadership," *American Economic Review*, 41(4), December 1951, 891-905.

McCallum, Bennett T. "The Development of Keynesian Macroeconomics," *American Economic Review*, 77(2), May 1987, 125-129.

________. "Are Bond-Financed Deficits Inflationary? A Ricardian Analysis," *Journal of Political Economy*, February 1984, 123-135.

Mean, G. "A Model of Consumer Durables," Treasury Academic Panel Paper AP(79)23, 1979.

Mishkin, Frederic S. "The Household Balance Sheet and the Great Depression," *Journal of Economic History*, 38(4), December 1978, 918-937.

________. "Illiquidity, Consumer Durable Expenditure, and Monetary Policy," *American Economic Review*, 66(3), September 1976, 642-654.

Modigliani, Franco. "Monetary Policy and Consumption: Linkages Via Interest Rate and Wealth Effects in the FMP Model," in *Consumer Spending and Monetary Policy: The Linkages*. Federal Reserve Bank of Boston Monetary Conference Series No. 5, 1971, 222-253.

________ and Albert Ando. "The Life Cycle Hypothesis of Saving," *American Economic Review*, 53(2), March 1963, 77-99.

Moore, Basil J. "The Endogenous Money Supply," *Journal of Post Keynesian Economics*, 10(3), Spring 1988, 372-385.

________. "How Credit Drives the Money Supply: The Significance of Institutional Developments," *Journal of Economic Issues*, 20(2), June 1986, 221-232.

________. "Contemporaneous Reserve Accounting: Can Reserves be Quantity-Constrained?" *Journal of Post Keynesian Economics*, 7(1), Fall 1984, 103-113.

________. "Monetary Factors," in *A Guide to Post Keynesian Economics*, A. Eichner, ed. New York: M. E. Sharpe, 1978, 120-138.

Norris, George W. "Note on Installment Credit," *Bulletin of the University of Kansas*, 30(14), 1926, 207-212.

Norton, Robert. "Citibank Wows the Consumer," *Fortune*, June 8, 1982, 47-54.

Patinkin, Don. "The Chicago Tradition, the Quantity Theory, and Friedman," *Journal of Money, Credit, and Banking*, 1(1), February 1969, 92-115.

Peterson, Ronald L. "Usury Laws and Consumer Credit: A Note," *Journal of Finance*, 38(4), September 1983, 1299-1304.

________. "The Impact of General Credit Restraint on the Supply of Commercial Bank Installment Credit," *Journal of Money, Credit, and Banking*, 8(5), November 1976, 527-535.

Projector, Dorothy S., and Gertrude S. Weiss. "Survey of Financial Characteristics of Consumers," *Federal Reserve Bulletin*, 53(2), March 1966, 96-104.

Seger, Martha. "Speech to the Committee of Banking, Finance, and Urban Affairs, U.S. House of Representatives, March 18, 1987," *Federal Reserve Bulletin*, 73(5), May 1987, 467-470.

Shay, Robert P. "Factors Affecting Price, Volume, and Credit Risk in the Consumer Finance Industry," *Journal of Finance*, 25(2), May 1970, 503-515.

________ and W. Dunkelberg. "Retail Store Credit Card Use in New York," in *Studies in Consumer Credit*, R. Shay, ed. Columbia University Graduate School of Business, 1975, 77-104.

Sims, Christopher. "Money, Income, and Causality," *American Economic Review*, 62(3), September 1972, 540-552.

Smith, James D., and Stephen Franklin. Estimates reported by the U.S. Bureau of the Census in the *Statistical Abstract of the United States*. Government Printing Office, 1975.

Smith, Paul F. "Pricing Policies on Consumer Loans at Commercial Banks," *Journal of Finance*, 40(2), March 1985, 517-525.

________. Tynan Smith, Alfred P. Johnson, Elsi T. Nelson, Katherine P. Reil, and Phillip M. Webster, "Revision of Consumer Credit Statistics," *Federal Reserve Bulletin*, 39(4), April 1953, 336-354.

Smith, Warren L. "Consumer Installment Credit: A Review Article," *American Economic Review*, 47(5), September 1957, 966-984.

Tapscott, T. R. "Consumer Installment Credit, 1980-1985," *Survey of Current Business*, 65(8), August 1985, 12-16.

Teeters, Nancy H. Statement to the Committee on Banking, Housing, and Urban Affairs, U.S. Senate, May 24, 1979. *Federal Reserve Bulletin*, 65(1), June 1979, 467-70.

Tobin, James. "A General Equilibrium Approach to Monetary Theory," *Journal of Money, Credit, and Banking*, 1(1), February 1969, 15-30.

________. "The Theory of Portfolio Selection," in *The Theory of Interest Rates*, F. Hahn and F. Brechling, eds. London: Macmillan, 1965.

________. "Liquidity Preference as Behavior Toward Risk," *Review of Economic Studies*, 25, February 1958, 65-86.

Williams, R. H. "Demand for Consumer Durables, Stock Adjustment Models, and Alternative Specifications of Stock Depletion," *Review of Economic Studies*, 39, September 1972, 977-1011.

Woglom, G. "A Reexamination of the Role of Stocks in the Consumption Function and the Transmission Mechanism," *Journal of Money, Credit, and Banking*, 12(4), May 1981, 479-490.

Wolken, John, "Geographic Market Delineation: A Review of the Literature," Staff Study, Federal Reserve Board, November 1984.

Zarnowitz, Victor, and Charlotte Boschon. "Cyclical Indicators: An Evaluation of New Leading Indexes," *Business Conditions Digest*, 75(5), May 1975, 5-19.

Index